GNVQ Into Practice

Edited by
LINDA GLOVER

Training and
Development Co-ordinator
for the
Southern Regional Council
for Education and Training

How was it for you?

CASSELL

Cassell
Wellington House, 125 Strand, London WC2R 0BB, England
215 Park Avenue South, New York, NY 10003, USA

© Linda Glover and contributors 1995

First published 1995

British Library Cataloguing-in-Publication Data
A catalogue record for this book is available from the British Library.

ISBN 0-304-33245-3 (paperback)

Typeset by York House Typographic Ltd, London
Printed and bound in Great Britain by the Bath Press

Contents

Contributors

Nick Bailey is GNVQ Co-ordinator, St Brendan's Sixth Form College, Bristol.

Anne Bourner is GNVQ Centre Co-ordinator, Manchester College of Arts and Technology.

Terry Cowham is Senior Vice-Principal, Manchester College of Arts and Technology.

Linda Glover is Training and Development Co-ordinator for the Southern Regional Council for Education and Training.

Richard Hewlett is Head of School, Languages, Leisure and Tourism, Gloucester College of Arts and Technology.

Jill Johnson is Lecturer in Business Studies, Gloucester College of Arts and Technology.

Tony Lau-Walker is Head of Division for Continuing Education and Professional Development, Guildford College of Further and Higher Education.

George Pattison is Curriculum Team Leader, St Chad's RC Comprehensive School, Runcorn.

Sylvia Willerton is Deputy Director of Sixth Form Studies, Wootton Bassett School.

Peter Wren is Head of Staff Development and Training, CENTRA.

Linda Wyatt is GNVQ Co-ordinator, Ferndown Upper School, Bournemouth.

Editor's Note

GNVQs have been designed in response to the May 1991 White Paper *Education & Training for the 21st Century*.

The primary aims were to increase education and training participation rates; remove the vocational–academic divide and hence facilitate parity of esteem; and to rationalize the vocational education and training provision which consisted of a myriad of qualifications and courses.

Approaching four years on, the progress made against these aims has confounded many. There is within the pages of this book much evidence of the energy, commitment and enthusiasm that have fuelled the development of the GNVQs. There is also much evidence of the difficulties, confusion and frustration that have been experienced by staff and students. However, that said, it is clear that those involved in the first phase of GNVQ, both staff and students, are proud of, and pleased with, their achievement.

The contributions within this book will provide readers with insights into all aspects of GNVQs – from cross-institution responses to vocational specific activities to core skill implementation to progression beyond GNVQ.

In Chapter 1 Peter Wren, Head of Staff Development and Training at CENTRA, the regional body for education and training in the north-west, provides readers with an introduction to GNVQs. What they are; who they are for; benefits for students; implications for staff and students. There are numerous newsletters, information leaflets and handbooks which describe the language, structure and implementation timetable of GNVQ. This chapter presumes that you have read these and now wish to explore the practical issues and gain an insight into the reality behind the theory.

In Chapter 2 Tony Lau-Walker, Head of Division for Continuing Education and Professional Development at Guildford College of

Further and Higher Education, has related how his college approached the issues raised by GNVQ and supported their development. From the general impact on FE of both GNVQ and Incorporation, Tony has given his account of the curriculum challenge and how the college has established good practice across the institution.

Terry Cowham, Senior Vice-Principal and Anne Bourner, GNVQ Centre Co-ordinator, at MANCAT, Manchester College of Arts and Technology, have titled Chapter 3 'Structure and Chaos: Introducing GNVQs as a Vehicle for Institutional Change'. Again the clear message is that GNVQs should not be seen as additional or peripheral to the mainstream curriculum. If there is an intention to respond to the demand for vocational education provision, the whole institution must be involved as well as each individual practitioner.

The first of the vocational contributions appears in Chapter 4 and is written by Sylvia Willerton, Deputy Director of Sixth Form Studies, GNVQ Co-ordinator for Art and Design, at Wootton Bassett School in Wiltshire. Wootton Bassett School gained national notice in 1994 as the school that produced the first GNVQ 'graduate' to gain entry into HE. The chapter graphically describes the experience of all those involved. It provides an honest view which does not minimize the difficulties, but provides a wealth of helpful pointers and confirms the positive and successful nature of the initiative. There is an additional section which looks at the impact of the introduction of all the GNVQ programmes on the school and its sixth form. This further emphasizes the fact that the ramifications of the introduction of GNVQs will be felt throughout the institution.

Chapter 5 is written by Nick Bailey, GNVQ Co-ordinator at St Brendan's Sixth Form College in Bristol. This narrative account of the experience of the college takes the reader from the initial stages where the difficulties experienced were because of a lack of clarity about the nature of the Business GNVQ. Many centres were 'diverted' by looking for commonality with existing vocational programmes, in this case the established BTEC Awards. By sharing those early confused days in the first year of the pilot and the subsequent strategies adopted, both successful and unsuccessful, new centres can, hopefully, avoid too many of the same pitfalls. The chapter confirms the optimism and enthusiasm of GNVQ 'providers' who, despite it all, finish very firmly on a positive note.

Chapter 6 by Linda Wyatt, GNVQ Co-ordinator, Ferndown Upper School, Bournemouth, provides a Health and Social Care perspective of GNVQ implementation. The chapter progresses from the decision to become a pilot, via the early misunderstanding of the nature of the award, to the practical strategies that were put in place to develop the programmes, plus clear guidance as to how the vocational staff have approached implementation. This chapter, too, finishes on a positive quotation from a student which clearly illustrates the benefits that GNVQ brings to students previously under-provided for in post-16 education.

Chapter 7 focuses on Leisure and Tourism GNVQs as implemented at GLOSCAT, Gloucester College of Arts and Technology, and is contributed by Richard Hewlett, who is Head of School, Languages, Leisure and Tourism. This highlights once again the need for a total institutional approach to GNVQ and also the need to set aside some of the old practices of established vocational education. The centres which have achieved most are those which have been able to support and develop their staff either to learn new skills or to cast aside their previous well-tried and trusted methods and strategies. Readers can follow the developmental process that the staff and provision at GLOSCAT went through and sample two of the activities produced for students. The change from broad sweep to specifically detailed activities is a potent illustration of the changes in practice that have occurred over the short life of the Leisure and Tourism GNVQ programme at GLOSCAT.

Chapter 8 by George Pattison, Curriculum Team Leader at St Chad's RC Comprehensive School in Runcorn, provides an account of this school's experience in implementing the Manufacturing GNVQ at Intermediate level. By bringing forward information from the first and second years of delivery there are many useful and practical pieces of advice for those considering their own institution's ability to deliver this GNVQ. There are also some useful insights as to the nature of the cohort for which this qualification could be appropriate. The value of ensuring practical reality for the vocational students comes through with particular clarity, as does the fascinating range of activities that can be made available for students' active learning.

Chapter 9 is contributed by Jill Johnson, lecturer in Business Studies at GLOSCAT and currently on secondment to manage the GLOSCAT/UCAS/UWE Project, 'Matching Advanced GNVQs to HE Programmes'. By taking the reader through the initial stages of planning for, working towards and applying for progression, a comprehensive picture is developed. This provides practical and essential guidance which will help you whether you be a manager, tutor, adviser, parent or student.

The figures in this book are reproduced with the permission of the institutions with which the contributors are associated.

As this book goes to print the time and tide of GNVQ is moving inexorably onwards. Whether you have already taken the 'plunge' or are still waiting for the 'dust to settle', these accounts of experiences during the first two years of GNVQs provide a wealth of information and insight.

LINDA GLOVER
Training & Development Co-ordinator
SRCET

Abbreviations

ABTA	Association of British Travel Agents
ADAR	Art and Design Admissions Registry
APL	Accreditation of Prior Learning
BA	Bachelor of Arts
BTEC	Business Technology Education Council
C&G/CGLI	City and Guilds (of London Institute)
CAD	Computer-Aided Design
CAR	Cumulative Assessment Record
CLAIT	Computer Literacy and Information Technology
COA	Cambridge Occupational Analysts Ltd
CPVE	Certificate of Pre-Vocational Education
Dip HE	Diploma in Higher Education
DOVE	Diploma of Vocational Education
FE	Further Education
FEFC	Further Education Funding Council
FEI	Further Education Institution
FEU	Further Education Unit
GATE	GNVQ Access to Higher Education
GCSE	General Certificate of Secondary Education
GEST	Grants for Education Support Training
GLOSCAT	Gloucester College of Arts and Technology
GNVQ	General National Vocational Qualification
HE	Higher Education
HEI	Higher Education Institution
HMI	Her Majesty's Inspector
HND	Higher National Diploma
IT	Information Technology
IV	Internal Verifier
MANCAT	Manchester College of Arts and Technology
MDF	Medium Density Fibre

MIS	Management Information System
NCVQ	National Council for Vocational Qualifications
NVQ	National Vocational Qualification
OFSTED	The Office for Standards in Education
PUSH	The Polytechnic and University Students' Handbook
RSA	Royal Society of Arts
TDLB	Training and Development Lead Body
TEC	Training and Enterprise Council
TQM	Total Quality Management
TVEI	Technical Vocational Education Initiative
UCAS	Universities and Colleges Admissions Service

PART ONE   Looking at GNVQ

Chapter 1

PETER WREN # An Introduction to GNVQs

What are GNVQs?

GNVQs are General National Vocational Qualifications and are intended to provide a third and vocational progression route as an additional choice to the well-established and traditional academic route of GCSEs, A levels and degrees, as well as the equally well-established but recently revised occupational route of NVQs (levels 1 to 5).

They are regarded as general because the knowledge, skills and understanding within them underpin the competence required to perform a wide range of occupational roles within each vocational area. In this way they differ from but are complementary to the occupational NVQs, which are much more specifically aligned with particular jobs but for which GNVQs provide an important grounding for future accelerated progression into and through the NVQ route. For this reason, GNVQs have been seen as an important feature of the 'accelerated' Modern Apprenticeship scheme.

They are seen as national as the awards are based upon national standards, or uniform specifications, accredited by the National Council for Vocational Qualifications (NCVQ). Regardless of the awarding body, the major content of each GNVQ (i.e. mandatory units and core skill units) is the same throughout England, Northern Ireland and Wales. The Isle of Man has also adopted these qualifications despite the fact that it is not subject to British Government legislation. Numerous countries overseas are also offering them as franchises from British colleges: these include Bahrain, France, Germany, Gibraltar, Hong Kong and Spain.

Interest has also been shown in GNVQs by Australia and New Zealand. In Scotland, which has a separate educational system from the rest of the United Kingdom, there are similar qualifications with

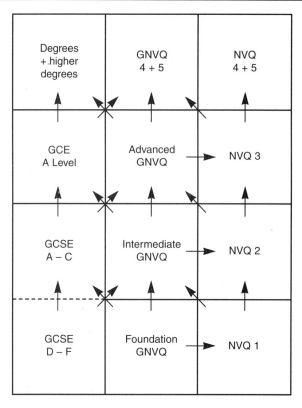

Figure 1.1 Possible
progression routes and
combinations for GNVQ
students.

a slightly different structure known as General Scottish Vocational Qualifications (GSVQs), accredited by SCOTVEC (the Scottish Vocational Education Council).

They are viewed as vocational because the specifications are directly related to the knowledge, skills and understanding which are required for working in any job within each vocational area. Thus they provide a background to and a strong foundation for making a choice of an occupation or career in the relevant vocational area.

Finally, they stand firmly as qualifications which are designed to establish themselves alongside both GCSEs/A levels and NVQs. This is not only as a separate and distinct progression route but also as a middle route. Candidates may move into this from the other two routes, out of it to either of the other two, or possibly combine with one of the other two (see Figure 1.1).

Who are GNVQs Intended for?

GNVQs, at the first three levels, have been designed specifically for students aged between 16 and 18 in full-time education as a counterpart to NVQs (at the first three levels) which have been designed for either trainees or employees in full-time employment but with part-time release for training.

They are intended for those students who:

(a) may not have decided as yet upon a specific occupation or career;
(b) may prefer a course which involves a more vocational (rather than academic) emphasis;
(c) may wish to combine a vocational qualification with additional GCSEs or an A level;
(d) may wish to combine a vocational qualification with units of an occupational qualification or a full occupational qualification;
(e) may develop better and become more thoroughly prepared for a higher education course through the teaching and learning approaches adopted in delivering GNVQs.

It is important to realise that, although GNVQs have been developed with full-time 16 to 18-year-old students in mind, their use is not solely restricted to this cohort. It is anticipated that the numbers of GNVQ students outside this specific group will grow rapidly and that these will include:

(a) Students aged 14 to 16 in Key Stage 4 of their schooling who will most probably complete a number of units of a GNVQ before moving on to achieve a full GNVQ at the same or a higher level in post-16 education. (This situation will be formalized in Part One GNVQ pre-16 by 1996.)
(b) Part-time students aged 16–18 who will still be required to complete the full GNVQ by using work-based projects to generate evidence. (No part-time GNVQ is available in the same way that BTEC have provided a part-time certificate as opposed to a full-time diploma with the certificate involving less work but at the same level as the diploma.)
(c) Adults will also be able to work towards GNVQs through full-time, part-time or open learning study routes. (In fact, the Advanced GNVQ in Management Studies is aimed at the post-18 group.)

Benefits to Students

GNVQs provide students with the opportunity to progress at their own pace and to work at their own level, whilst at the same time having their progress both recorded and accredited. This can mean that, for many otherwise disillusioned or demoralized students, GNVQs provide a highly motivating learning programme. The format and approach of GNVQs enable students to develop and demonstrate their ability to learn. This is particularly true of the core skills which are improved through their application in the vocational context. Achievement in GNVQ is evidenced in the portfolio, and the comprehensive coverage ensures that the completion of a full GNVQ demonstrates an overall ability related to the knowledge, understanding and skills required in that area. Transition at 16 and 18 should be eased by this confidence in full coverage which provides a complete profile of a student's ability. Students are also encouraged to develop self-confidence, responsibility, investigative/research skills, self-study skills and, through self-assessment, an understanding of their own strengths and weaknesses. Work in vocational areas should also assist in producing much more informed career choices.

Implications for Deliverers and Students

From the experience of the pilot centres and of GNVQ centres, it has become clear that a range of issues concerning the implementation of GNVQs needs to be taken into serious consideration *prior* to the beginning of each year's programme. It must be stressed that these issues concern the whole institution, not just a small group within it (e.g. the GNVQ delivery team). As such they must be tackled as institutional concerns, brought about by but not restricted to GNVQs and the staff responsible for them or the students working towards them. These issues are outlined and discussed below.

Institutional plan

The centre must initially (and probably provisionally) decide in which vocational areas it will offer GNVQs. With the present proposal of at least 14 vocational areas to be covered by GNVQs, it is highly likely that most centres would wish to be selective in their choice. Much would depend upon the size of the centre, what courses it has previously offered and the potential for growth which the centre expects to be realized by GNVQs.

The next decision would concern the levels at which each GNVQ is to be offered. The reasons for this decision may be very similar to those stated above, but would also include an analysis of the ability range of the potential candidates and the payment of attention to suitable progression routes for candidates, within and beyond the institution.

Having decided upon the vocational areas and levels, the centre will need to consider which of the three awarding bodies (i.e. BTEC,

City and Guilds or RSA) it wishes to register with for its GNVQs. Since each awarding body requires a centre to be subject to a centre-approval process, it makes some sense for a centre to decide upon operating with one body and one body only. However, certain large centres may be quite prepared to allow individual departments to make their own choice of awarding body. Unlike the choice of GCSE or GCE boards, the decision upon the GNVQ awarding body is not based upon the differences in syllabuses and possibly in assessment methods. All three GNVQ awarding bodies offer virtually the same GNVQ specifications at each level (this is true of the mandatory and core skill unit at all levels and the optional units at Foundation level). The only variation in specifications occurs in the optional and additional units at Intermediate and Advanced level. Certainly the assessment methods to be used are the same as they must adhere to national standards. The decision on which awarding body to work with may depend a little upon their respective fee levels or their different administrative arrangements (e.g. recording systems and documentation). Usually centres select a particular awarding body for historical reasons – that is, it is most common for centres to continue to work with the awarding body, for GNVQs, with which it has previously worked for other schemes (e.g. BTEC First and National Diplomas, City and Guilds DOVE or RSA CLAIT).

Curriculum plan

When introducing GNVQs, centres need to be clear about the rationale for this. The expense and commitment which are required for any curriculum innovation necessitate that centres take sound decisions based upon thorough consultation with and advice from the various bodies and organizations involved with GNVQ developments. It is important that centres do not act upon a sudden whim or seek to jump upon the current bandwagon. Certainly, current guidance is that centres which do not have a history of vocational education should delay implementation until 1995/96 at the earliest.

Reasons for introducing GNVQ will vary from centre to centre but there are particular ones which recur across the country. In post-16 education, many centres have replaced GCSE resit programmes with Intermediate GNVQs. The reasons for this are obvious. Many people are fully aware of the notoriously unsuccessful nature of resit programmes. Many students have spent an entire year undergoing the somewhat demoralizing experience of repeating the work undertaken in Year 11 in school only to find that they have made little or no progress. For such students, Intermediate GNVQs provide a refreshing change and essentially give the students a new start and an alternative route into Advanced GNVQs. Likewise, for weaker students who would have no great incentive or desire to attempt to improve E–G grades, the Foundation GNVQs offer a different approach to learning and the advantage of recognizing positive achievement through unit accreditation and credit accumulation.

Advanced GNVQs may be introduced as either a replacement for previous vocational awards (e.g. BTEC National) which are being phased out in those areas where GNVQs are available or an alternative to GCE A levels. Where centres are replacing old awards the timing of GNVQ implementation varies from introducing GNVQs as soon as they are available to waiting until the previous award finally disappears. In the case of offering an alternative to A levels, many centres have looked closely at areas with no closely corresponding A level (e.g. Leisure and Tourism or Health and Social Care as opposed to Art and Design or Business).

Centres may wish to offer students the possibility of combining an Advanced GNVQ with a GCE A level or an Intermediate or Foundation GNVQ with a number of GCSEs. Any combination with A level should ensure that the subjects do not overlap but instead complement each other (e.g. avoid GNVQ Art and Design with A-level Art or GNVQ Business with A-level Business Studies, instead choose GNVQ Art and Design with A-level History or GNVQ Business with A-level Economics). Offering GCSEs with GNVQ should avoid resit GCSEs as far as possible, with the exception of Maths and English which remain as important requirements by both employers and higher education. It is much more encouraging for students to attempt what to them would be new subjects at GCSE, such as Economics, Psychology, Sociology, Italian, Russian, etc.

At Key Stage 4, the introduction of GNVQs or GNVQ units may be seen as a means of broadening the curriculum by offering Foundation and Intermediate levels across the full ability range, thus providing a vocational taster in preparation for post-16 education or training.

Timetabling

Centres need to bear in mind that although GNVQs have been developed on an outcomes model and therefore different students will achieve those outcomes at a different rate, experience has led to certain recommendations being made about time allocation for

GNVQ delivery. It is recommended that centres provide approximately 14–16 hours per week for a full GNVQ (at any of the three levels assuming a one-year programme for Foundation and Intermediate and two years for Advanced). This recommendation is based upon calculations from a concurrent model allowing two hours per week per vocational unit (six units = 12 hours), one hour per week per core skill unit (2–3 hours depending on whether time is allocated to communication) and possibly one hour per week for tutorial support. This renders a total of 14 hours or 16 (including communication and tutorial). It is debatable as to how much of this timetabled provision should be regarded as class contact time. Many centres have successfully timetabled work placement/experience, assignments, project work/research, drop-in workshops, use of open learning packages and access to IT facilities into this allocation.

It is important that centres timetable blocks of time for GNVQ work. The activity-based nature of GNVQ makes it unsuitable for lessons of 30–45 minutes, the possible exception being for core skills or tutorial support. For the vocational units, lessons should be no shorter than one hour and there is a preference for whole mornings or afternoons in order to allow for project or investigative work to be carried out thoroughly.

Group size varies from the minimum number which a centre is prepared to accept as cost-effective (in many cases allowing some leeway for a new qualification to get off the ground) to the maximum number which the nature of GNVQ work, access to equipment (e.g. computers) or safety regulations will allow. Experience has shown that this may mean that groups have from six to 25 students although the norm lies in the 12–18 range.

Staffing

It is important that the members of the GNVQ delivery team have experience of teaching on vocational programmes. In many cases, it would prove useful for staff to have industrial or commercial or professional experience (e.g. travel agency, tourist board or leisure centre experience for Leisure and Tourism; a nursing or social work background for Health and Social Care). Where members of staff are drawn from a traditional, academic teaching background, it is essential to provide a programme of staff induction covering the philosophy, language and structure of GNVQs, appropriate teaching and learning styles of the GNVQ students, the integration of core skills and developing a team approach to assessment. No members of staff should be expected to deliver a full GNVQ on their own. Delivery requires teams of at least two in order to provide the breadth and expertise to cover all the units.

A coherent and successful GNVQ programme usually requires the fulfilment of two key roles, i.e. co-ordination and programme management. These roles may be combined into one post but in large institutions they may be carried out by two or more people. The programme manager should be a senior manager in the centre in order that the appropriate priority is given to the timetabling needs of GNVQs, decisions on the size of the blocks of teaching time, provision of core skills support and tutorial support for student portfolio building. It is vital for the success of programmes that the manager can ensure the required level of provision and resourcing.

The GNVQ co-ordinator may also be the programme manager in small centres, but in larger institutions this role may be fulfilled by a programme or course leader. The significance of this role is that there is an essential need for one person to liaise with the awarding bodies in order to ascertain the latest developments in GNVQs and to disseminate information to staff as promptly as is practical. The co-ordinator will also liaise with outside agencies such as industry, work placement providers, higher education, NCVQ and the local community.

Candidates

There are no formal entry requirements for students to access GNVQ programmes; however, a degree of guidance has been provided on the minimum achievements which centres would expect candidates to have in order to indicate a strong possibility of success in GNVQs. At post-16 level it is suggested that:

- Advanced GNVQ requires at least 4/5 GCSEs at grade C;
- Intermediate GNVQ requires at least 2 GCSEs at grade D;
- Foundation GNVQ requires at least 2 GCSEs at grade G.

In Key Stage 4, the suggestion is to look closely at achievement in the core-skill areas in Key Stage 3 (this would particularly apply to English and Maths) and to look at the potential for achievement of GCSE grades.

Inevitably decisions have to be made on the appropriate GNVQ levels for individual candidates. These decisions may be deferred beyond the immediate start of the course in order to allow students in a mixed-level group to demonstrate their capability and potential. Examination results in dissimilar qualifications may not be the most accurate predictors of success in GNVQs.

Induction for candidates is vital and may be of an extended period of time. It is suggested that the induction programme should provide an introduction to the GNVQ learning programme and its contents, familiarization with the structure and terminology of GNVQs and the issuing of specifications to students. It is important to make clear to students such details as the sequencing of units and how they will be timetabled and staffed. Students must understand that the active-learning strategy places a responsibility upon them to develop and improve their own learning.

It is useful for centres to undertake some diagnostic assessment and accreditation of any prior achievement before allowing students to embark upon some sample learning activities in their chosen GNVQ area (or across a number of areas if required). At this point it may be appropriate to introduce the guidance and counselling service which centres establish in order to support the candidates in meeting the requirements made of them to achieve a full GNVQ. Sample learning opportunities may also involve the students in developing basic study skills such as research/investigative techniques; planning, generating and collecting evidence; presenting information and team-building and group work skills.

It is possible for this work to be followed up by more specific work on action planning and on portfolio building. Students should be familiarized with the appropriate awarding body record-keeping documentation, as well as the test arrangements and the operation of the grading criteria.

The process of action planning is an important activity for students. The centre needs to decide upon how and when to deliver the strategy chosen and the significance placed upon the linking up of the completion of the units with the availability of the external tests. Once the year plan for the centre is in place, students may action-plan within this framework. The main purpose of student action planning is to draw up both short-term and long-term outlines of how sufficient and appropriate evidence will be produced for taking grading themes and grading criteria into account.

Students are encouraged to think and work independently. There is an emphasis in the GNVQ specifications upon activities with guidance, support and some teaching provided by staff as opposed to structured instruction. Good guidance and monitoring are essential to ensure that students produce evidence which is relevant to the performance criteria in the required elements.

Evidence and record keeping

The evidence produced by students must cover everything: all units, elements, performance criteria and range statements. The evidence is presented in a 'portfolio' which may vary from an A4 file to a box or crate (e.g. for three-dimensional objects in Art and Design or Manufacturing). Pieces of work may be repeated or replaced but not omitted if they are the only examples of coverage of certain performance criteria. Apart from written pieces of work on paper, portfolio evidence may include paintings, sculptures, castings, wooden furniture, video and audio recordings, computer disks and wall displays. The students have responsibility for looking after their own work, but most centres store it for them in order to safeguard it. However, this decision does raise the issue of finding adequate and available storage space.

For the portfolio, it is essential that a clear index and cross-referencing system is employed in order to ensure that the contents are comprehensively listed and that all of the units, elements, performance criteria and range statements are covered. A clear system greatly assists the processes of internal and external verification.

It is regarded as important that centres develop an institutional approach to portfolio building, administrative procedures and record keeping based upon awarding body guidelines and documentation. It is advisable for the recording of evidence to be carried out by students on a regular basis (i.e. weekly rather than monthly or termly).

Assessment

Assessment of the evidence produced by the student is carried out by the vocational tutor and takes place against the achievement of the appropriate performance criteria. It is because of this crucial role as assessors that centres are required by the awarding bodies to ensure that all GNVQ staff assess to the standards laid down in the TDLB units D32 and D33. To encourage staff to work towards the achievement of those units and ensure that a minimum number of staff possess these units by the completion of the first full year of a centre's GNVQ programme, the centre needs to draw up its own action plan.

Internal verification of the assessment is also carried out by centre staff across possibly the whole centre, and certainly across vocational areas. Centres require at least two internal verifiers, as internal verifiers are not allowed to verify their own assessments.

Internal verifiers are required to work to the standards in the TDLB units D33 and D34.

External verification of centres and their assessments is carried out by external verifiers, as representatives of the awarding bodies. It is useful to recognize that the external verifiers not only fulfil the role of external verification and reporting back to the awarding bodies but also are expected to provide information, advisory and support services to centres both during visits and between visits (of which they make three per year). This is part of the requirement placed upon them to meet the standards in the TDLB units D33 and D35.

The centre must also make institutional plans for dealing with the external tests. These are available for each tested mandatory unit at each of the testing opportunities during the year as well as the resit opportunity in the autumn term. It is up to the programme manager or GNVQ co-ordinator to ensure that candidates are entered for all the tests for which they are ready at every opportunity. This may affect the timing of the completion of a unit (i.e. just before a testing opportunity appears) or the sequence of units (e.g. delivering mandatory before optional units) in order to increase the number of opportunities available for certain units.

Core skills

Ideally, the delivery and assessment of core skills should be carried out by the vocational tutors; however, in practice, it is much more likely that specialist core-skills staff will be used. It is important that these staff fully understand the GNVQ requirements and that they are involved in the GNVQ team. The work of the core-skills specialists not only includes them in teaching their particular area (e.g. Application of Number, Communication and Information Technology), possibly for one hour a week, but also in diagnostic testing of weaknesses in specific core-skills areas and providing additional support to all those students who require it. They will also be responsible for liaising with the vocational tutors in order to agree upon how the core skills will be assessed within the context of vocational assessment activities. These may require students to have frequent access to IT equipment in order to produce evidence of using word processing, databases and spreadsheets.

This chapter was written to give the reader the background to GNVQs. The following chapters will give you the opportunity to hear how the practice has worked out in a cross-section of post-16 providers.

Chapter 2

TONY LAU-WALKER # Further Education and GNVQ

How one college – Guildford College of Further and
Higher Education – approached the issues raised by
GNVQ and supported its development

The Impact on Further Education

At the original briefing sessions for the GNVQ Phase I programmes
in March 1992, many college representatives expressed the general
view that here was yet another new curriculum initiative – how
long would it last? What few realized in those early meetings were
the real size and potential of the GNVQ. For further education (FE)
it has meant a change in the nature of FE itself. With 1,500 centres
registered to deliver GNVQs at the start of the first year of the
unrestricted delivery of the qualification, and a take-up of over
80,000 candidates, GNVQs clearly represented big business and
colleges not only had to take this new curriculum initiative seriously, they faced a much greater range of rival provision entering
into the marketplace they once monopolized.

It would seem that the take-up of GNVQs in schools has had more
impact on vocational education in the curriculum than the £200
million spent under the TVEI programme. A rapidly expanding
school-based vocational provision will increasingly prove a threat to
college enrolments – not merely in terms of overall size of market
share available to them but also in the quality of the candidates
available – as schools, with an eye on league table results, appear
keen to keep the better candidates for their own programmes.
Moreover, the introduction of GNVQs coincided with the incorporation of colleges and has given Sixth Form colleges an unexpected
opportunity to level the playing field with Technical colleges in
terms of the range of vocationally orientated curriculum offered by
them. Very quickly the Sixth Form college programme of full-time
study has begun to resemble that of the local Technical college, and
where the Sixth Form college has close links with feeder schools this
gives them obvious advantages over their rivals.

For FE in general the introduction of GNVQ has created a far more competitive environment with more providers than ever before, as well as a more urgent need to develop an effective marketing strategy to successfully differentiate its own provision from that of the new providers in the market. Indeed, the marketing strategy for GNVQs is the most complex problem facing colleges which – unlike schools – have no captive audience pre-16 to cultivate, and which also appear, on the surface at least, to have lost their unique selling point of providing vocational programmes which offer progression to employment or higher education. Not that most FE colleges anticipated such a situation when the pilot phase began in 1992/93. For many staff and most curriculum managers the situation was seen as one of replacing like with like – a view BTEC themselves actively promoted.[1] Discontinuing BTEC Nationals and First Diplomas for BTEC GNVQs was emotionally painful for staff attached to qualifications most felt worked well, but as a curriculum strategy it was a process which seemed to require little management attention or support for the staff involved in such changes. The consequence of this misperception has had an enormous impact on the workload of main grade lecturers and programme managers and in terms of opportunity costs for colleges has exacerbated the strategic position of many colleges in their local vocational education marketplace.

The Curriculum Challenge

With the introduction of the GNVQ curriculum not only have we witnessed a significant change in 'who' delivers vocational education but, just as important, we have a major revision of 'what' is delivered and 'how' it is to be delivered and assessed.

The GNVQ curriculum has been deliberately designed as a broad-based vocational education. It is not vocational preparation and it has no tight specific job focus – that is the NVQ design. This broader-based design represents a change of emphasis for many college staff who are accustomed to a more focused vocational programme; for them the GNVQ appears caught between two stools – vocational preparation and general education. Indeed, one colleague at first sight of the GNVQ draft specifications felt that FE was being turned into a general education programme and her specialism would no longer be required.

GNVQs are described as a foundation of study on which to build.[2] Made up of a range of units which have different functions within the overall scheme – mandatory, option, core and additional studies units – the curriculum is intended to provide learners with a range of choices to be exercised depending upon their progression route and their initial learning needs. Such a scheme fits well with counselling and guidance, action planning, primary learning goals and additional units of study which now comprise the funding methodology of the Further Education Funding Council, though in practice staff have great difficulty creating and implementing a flexible provision which realizes these ideals. Those difficulties are partly based upon resourcing constraints but mainly on attitudinal constraints which stem from either an unwillingness to allow or encourage student-based choice within programmes, or a lack of recognition of the value or appropriateness of choice.

At Guildford preparation for Phase I delivery began in the Summer term, supported by some development time releasing staff from class contact. The four vocational teams were tasked by their managers to replace BTEC First and National Diplomas with GNVQ 2 and 3. They continued their work during the summer break to have a programme ready for September – even though there would be no core-skill specifications available until October. However, after the first two months of the Phase I implementation, staff accepted that something very new and basically radical could now be offered to students but they had not properly prepared themselves or their programme design to realize the opportunities represented by the new curriculum design. In their attempts to resolve the implementation issues the programme managers and the GNVQ co-ordinator examined the GNVQ in terms of the curriculum opportunities it offered students and examined the institutional blocks to the realization of these opportunities.

The following list of significant features of the new GNVQ design summarized the view of staff at Guildford College after two months of delivery and raised important delivery issues which would need significant staff and curriculum development to address adequately.[3]

- **_Broad-based_ vocational education**
  Staff need to widen their area of expertise and become more generalist within an occupational area.
- **Specified as _outcomes_ to be achieved**
  Learning can be accredited at a pace suitable to each learner – hence cohort programming becomes more difficult, resource-based learning is more appropriate and access to frequent and varied assessment opportunities is essential.

- **Made up of a number of *units***
  The move to integrate knowledge across a range of units encouraged by BTEC until now becomes less useful as unit accreditation becomes more important.

- **Have mandatory, option, additional and core-skill units**
  A range of types of units, assessed differently and with different roles to play in the programme of each learner, reinforces the move away from integration and requires the centre to develop a clear rationale as to the relationship between each unit and the role it has to play both in the programme of the learner and the portfolio of the centre itself.

- **Credits may be *accumulated***
  Part achievement is more relevant and realistic for some learners and this choice means that a delay in full certification is an available option. It is also possible to transfer achievement from one centre to another perhaps to attain the right option or additional studies to complete the programme.

- **Awarded for *achievement*, irrespective of time taken or mode of learning**
  The potential to provide variable speeds of achievement – fast track and slow track and to vary the number of units achieved (the highest so far attempted being 23 units) – demands a very flexible approach and creative programme management.

- **Portfolio of evidence used for grading**
  The complexity of grading offers a short term[4] challenge of how to provide formative feedback without prejudicing the summative grading activity but seeks to achieve a more sophisticated evaluation of the candidate as a learner rather on the degree of knowledge acquired, thus offering a far more complex assessment than rival qualifications.

- ***External* tests for mandatory units**
  Seen as a politically essential feature of the design but in many ways tangential to the delivery and assessment design in the rest of the programme. Essentially a feature needing careful management by the delivery team otherwise it would take over the whole programme design leading the learners and deliverers rather than playing a confirmatory role as anticipated. The more frequent the test availability the better able to achieve a low profile on the programme.

- **A genuine *alternative* to academic qualifications for progression**

  Awareness and acceptance of the qualification by HE would require considerable efforts to link, liaise and inform HE departments likely to receive our students – and the additional studies units and choices would help to establish and develop this dialogue.
- **An alternative *route* into employment as well as HE**

  As with HE, awareness and acceptance would depend on links and liaison. Both the work experience and the additional studies choices would be useful mechanisms for establishing dialogue.

The conclusion of the implementation review team was simple but far-reaching – GNVQs properly delivered represent choice: essentially student choice and student empowerment. As a broad foundation a GNVQ required action planning to create specific pathways to higher education or work which suited each individual learner. Such a curriculum offer required counselling and guidance to ensure that students were able to make informed decisions throughout the programme, and it also meant staff development to enable staff to support such decision-making and to create flexible programmes which allow such decisions to be made. A second, and related, perspective was also taken – that additional studies was a central feature of GNVQs and not a marginal one. Additional studies provided a double benefit. They exercised and enhanced students' ability to choose and helped the college to make a better curriculum offer to potential students as it had a wider choice than their competitor institutions. Unlike existing qualifications being replaced by GNVQs, the GNVQ was not a sealed unit self-contained and offered as a complete package. It was a foundation to be added to where necessary. If it was to be used by a learner as a preparation for employment then suitable units of NVQs could be undertaken alongside the GNVQ. If the learner intended to undertake further study then appropriate additional studies units or an A level could be selected to complete the preparation for progression. The GNVQ could be used in combination with most of the other curriculum provision in the college, which enhanced the breadth of opportunity for the individual learner as well as for the college (see Figure 2.1).

With the emphasis on choice and the importance of additional studies the college was faced with curriculum development issues at both a local and a strategic level. A replacement strategy of allowing delivery teams to design new programmes to deliver discrete courses as of old was no longer appropriate. A review and rationalization of the whole curriculum portfolio was required and, indeed, a

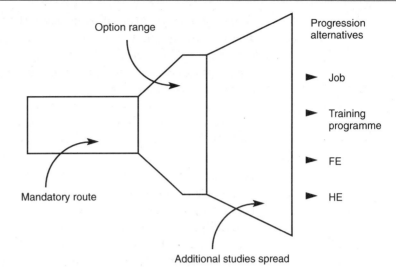

Figure 2.1   GNVQ structure.

process of re-engineering the whole institution was a medium-term consequence of the strategic implications of this focus on choice. Senior managers needed to be aware of these issues and be ready to provide a broader development context and clear set of priorities for their delivery teams if the full potential of GNVQs was to be realized by the college to successfully differentiate its curriculum offer in the newly competitive environment. During the spring and summer terms of 1992/93 this is exactly what the college aimed to achieve.

Establishing Good Practice

The college set up a cross-college development programme which focused upon the eight vocational areas involved in Phase I and preparing for Phase II. This group was programme managers and team members for Advanced and Intermediate programmes. Their brief was to address the demands of this new curriculum and set out to consider the blocks to realizing opportunities contained within the GNVQ. By combining staff from those teams already delivering the GNVQ with those preparing for it, the intention was to discuss delivery issues, reflect on experience and establish good practice in a shortened time-frame.

Remarkably the staff quickly stopped identifying the differences between their vocational areas and concentrated on the commonality of the shared framework. It was also encouraging to see that, in the face of what became clear as wide-ranging change, staff were very open about the difficulties they were experiencing and the fears they had concerning their conditions of work, as well as the future shape of the vocational education that would be delivered. The group were given the explicit brief to make decisions about the structure and rationale of the GNVQ offer which the college would make for 1993/94, as long as those decisions were adhered to across all the vocational areas.

Simultaneously, senior managers were carefully briefed by the GNVQ co-ordinator as to the implications of the introduction of GNVQs and the kind of support needed by staff to optimize the changes to improve the curriculum offer to the general public. A two-year rolling programme of change was established which was fuelled by the cross-college development group. By the Easter break this group had established a common framework for GNVQ design and delivery at the college, and in the summer term they identified broader institutional development needs to be undertaken to remove broader organizational barriers to change and allow the realization of potential delivery benefits already identified. Throughout this process the senior managers encouraged this wave of re-engineering and provided funds to achieve the changes identified.

The major breakthrough for staff came with agreement on a timetable template (see Figure 2.2) designed to realize the element of choice and a wide range of additional studies for GNVQ candidates. The template was a skeleton rather than a complete programme design, to allow teams to handle their mandatory programmes in a way which best utilized their available staff and rooms. The two principles of its design were access to assessment and individual programmes:

- to spread the load of external tests – hence the introduction of the semester system;
- to make a clear commitment to unit delivery which enhances student access to a range of achievements rather than a blanket of integrated course delivery;
- to enable fast tracking and full GNVQ achievement in one year;
- to allow students to retake units and to choose a wider range of options than one cohort could sustain.

The template in Figure 2.2 below represents a Monday to Friday distribution of unit delivery which leaves Tuesday and Thursday in Year 1 as the focus for option and additional studies – including core-skill support. One point which tested staff's creativity was the concept that after running the programme for one year there were always two years of the programme running simultaneously; therefore both years' range of units are available to students at the start of any one year. Hence with this template a new student could undertake all the mandatories in one year or mix any proportion of mandatory, option and additional studies units they felt appropriate. As the college offers a wide range of one-year A levels most students could fit an A level into the second year of their programme if they followed the template chronologically – though given the range of additional studies available less than 30 per cent of advanced students do so.

	Year 1		Year 2	
	Semester 1	Semester 2	Semester 1	Semester 2
	Mandatory unit	Mandatory unit	Options Directed study	Additionals Work experience
	Options Directed study	Additionals Work experience	Mandatory unit	Mandatory unit
	Mandatory unit	Mandatory unit	Options Directed study	Additionals Work experience
	Options Directed study	Additionals Work experience	Options Directed study	Additionals Work experience
	Mandatory unit	Mandatory unit	Options Directed study	Additionals Work experience

Figure 2.2 Cross-college timetable template.

The ability to think creatively about timetable design and progression routes is always hemmed in by practical resource constraints, but it would appear that the biggest barrier is inertia and custom and practice. Senior and middle managers are as prone to these restrictions as the delivery teams. However, working as a group and focusing on principles rather than historical details the staff soon generated a range of potential opportunities offered by the GNVQ design which required a far more flexible timetable approach which the template represented. Whereas cohort progression is traditionally expected to start on the left-hand side of the template and move *en masse* to the right-hand side at the same pace – except for the drop-outs – staff had now created the opportunity for students to start at the top of the template and work their way down through a pathway of units they choose – with curriculum and career guidance from their tutors. Such guidance could start at interview so that recruitment ceased to be a selection exercise and became a marketing activity, which had a serious implication for the college's admissions practice.

This flexible approach emphasizes the 'programme' concept rather than the 'course' – units are to be picked up in a different order depending on the student's action plan. Part-time GNVQs can also benefit from this template approach, extending the units on offer with evening provision so that full-time students can fast-track even quicker and part-time programmes can take advantage of the resources available to the more viable full-time recruitment. Indeed, the real basis of wide-ranging choice as presented in Figure 2.1 depends upon generating cohorts of considerable size and then handling creatively the resourcing they attract. It was agreed in our planning group that 70 to 120 per intake would be an appropriate target for a medium-sized college such as ours, and this represents a vast difference to the groups of 10 or 20 most schools and smaller colleges have been working with. Intakes can be increased in size for planning purposes if part-time and full-time 1st and 2nd years are pooled – again, there is a need to encourage creative curriculum planning in staff who are too quick to break intakes into discrete small groups where choice becomes economically unviable. Moreover, a greater range of option units can be run if more students are taking them as additional studies, either from other vocational areas in cross-college provision or from within the same area. The creation of larger intake sizes may also have implications for the portfolio of programmes offered, and some vocational areas have rationalized the range of programmes offered to encourage the larger GNVQ cohort.

The introduction of the half-year semester system into the template spread the examination opportunities across the year so that the summer focus of external tests was definitely discouraged. It also introduced initially unseen opportunities such as the January intake and a half-yearly review process. The end of each semester provides an important review focus to decide whether action plans have been fully achieved, where they need revision and if units need to be retaken. It gives students the opportunity to have a first semester free of any additional units so that they can achieve a solid result on the mandatory programme and plan their option choice and additional studies programme effectively. It also gives staff a twice-yearly deadline to ensure students achieve all their internal assessments before progressing to another set of semester units. Finally, it also allows for students to make an orderly transfer between GNVQs if they wish; to revisit some units, without having to retake a whole term's work again; to get extra core-skills support; change work experience placements; and, most important for the college, new students are able to enter the system in a properly supported way at time other than September without having to arrive in sufficient numbers to form a discrete cohort. Indeed the system has the benefit of generating extra income for the college – not only by creating more recruitment opportunities but also by generating a higher rate of take-up for additional studies units. Most advanced students undertake a programme of between 16 and 20 units.

By the end of the first year, considering the experience of the delivery teams and the discussions and decisions of the planning group, the commitment to the 'choice model' as depicted in Figures 2.1 and 2.2 led to the following recommendation on resource allocations for all Advanced GNVQs:

- 45 per cent of programme hours to be focused on Mandatory Unit delivery;
- 20 per cent of programme hours to be focused on Option Unit delivery;
- 10 per cent of programme hours to be used for Individual Action Planning and guidance tutorials;
- 25 per cent of programme hours to be focused on Additional Studies provision – including option units, additional studies units, some core-skill support, in-fill places on existing non GNVQ provision, and discrete vocationally specific short courses.

Now that FEFC's funding methodology allows for extra funds for additional studies units then this formula can be resourced with less of a squeeze upon the mandatory programme.

There are literally more resources available for the additional-enriched programme! One consequence of encouraging additional studies has been the rapid growth in students undertaking GCSE English and Maths retakes to improve their grade profile. This did not happen with BTEC National recruits as students were generally not encouraged to mix and match general education qualifications with vocational areas. The bonus for the student wishing to progress to Higher Education – according to Judith Compton, the GATE Project Director[5] – is that selection for progression is significantly affected by the GCSE profile and the number and relevance of the additional units achieved.

Building on Good Practice

The decisions as to what constituted good practice based upon the college's own experience, as well as the fact finding from other centres, led to clear priorities for the following year which had a logical sequence of reviews and reforms relevant to delivery teams and senior managers in equal degrees. The emphasis on choice and the larger cohort sizes encouraged delivery teams to develop a better tracking system and a more structured and strengthened tutorial support provision. For the same reason senior managers needed to review the curriculum portfolio, to rationalize provision and encourage the development of more centralized and generic threshold services. The tracking of an individual student's learning goals and recording of on-programme achievement required a much more structured system which the cross-college team devised to fit all the GNVQs, but this in itself had an impact on the central MIS arrangements which needed revision to fit FEFC requirements. The GNVQ pattern of action-planning review and recording fitted neatly into the FEFC on-entry, on-programme, on-exit pattern and encouraged a tight fit between the college's GNVQ development and the rest of the MIS system (see Figure 2.3).

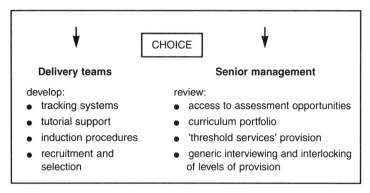

Figure 2.3   Support systems for student choice.

The tracking paperwork – an extensive 12 sheets per student – developed by a cross-college team and adopted and operated by all GNVQ teams, had shown the need for an ongoing tutorial support system to use the paperwork with students and provide the guidance central to the curriculum structure. Moreover, the larger cohorts also needed a stronger tutorial role to provide individual learning support and a more personal focus for individual help and referral that a smaller cohort size might take for granted in the programme manager. Balancing size with individual support was seen as a key issue to be resolved before the marketing of the larger programmes. A special two-day training programme was devised to turn out effective 'personal mentors' – the phrase we now used to identify GNVQ tutors, well-versed in the use of tracking documentation, portfolio management and grading criteria. By changing their name it was hoped that staff who had been tutors for years on other programmes would be able to leave their historical practices behind and adopt the new priorities and procedures relevant to GNVQ. They become the main referral point for the student within the college, connecting them with counselling services, learner support, core-skills workshops, careers guidance and finance.

Throughout his or her time on the GNVQ programme the student is now linked to one mentor whose role is to review progress and negotiate the action plan with the learner. He or she helps the learner complete the tracking documentation, provide guidance for their portfolio building, provide support when there are difficulties with assessment, complete any progression reference which may be required and, at all times, will act as an advocate in the academic interests of the learner. Resourced to provide a staff–tutee ratio in single figures, the mentor is now seen as an important role whose relationship with, and support for, the learner is crucial for the success of the programme. This is reflected in the mentor training programme designed for staff to understand the role thoroughly and to develop several key skills to make the most effective use of the time available for the role.

Promoting Quality

If the central role in the programme for maintaining the quality of the experience from the consumer's point of view – whether learner, parent or employer – is that performed by the personal mentor, this is balanced from the examination board – and from the College staff's perspective – by the internal verifier role. Though the college has established a three-year programme to accredit the relevant staff with NCVQ-prescribed TDLB Assessor Awards (D32, D33 and D34) the real change of culture within the delivery teams has come with the operation of the internal verifier following guidelines agreed by the programme managers halfway through the first year. These guidelines (included below) are something of an ideal but their comprehensiveness puts the internal verifier into a central position not only to inspect standards being set but also to develop both the process of the team's delivery and its assessment output.

GNVQ Internal Verification Guidelines

The internal verifier is responsible for inducting all assessors and candidates involved in the programme into the verification process so that the aims and mechanism of the process are fully understood. The internal verifier is also responsible for ensuring that all assessment documentation is properly maintained and submitted to the Awarding Body.

The internal verification process will be the essential quality assurance mechanism to ensure that assessments on GNVQ programmes are valid, reliable and sufficient.

Validity

- The assessment programme will be checked by the internal verifier to ensure that an agreed monitoring procedure is followed to establish validity of assessment activity to criteria being assessed.
- The setting of end tests to complete a module or unit of GNVQ which is not covered by external tests will also be subject to internal verification.
- All assessment activities need to be planned in advance and monitored by the internal verifier to ensure that both comprehensive coverage and sufficiency of opportunity are present in the assessment programme of each GNVQ.

Reliability

- Standardization of assessment results as well as accuracy and sufficiency of feedback to candidates will be periodically reviewed as part of the internal verification process. The internal verifier will monitor the second marking of assessment activities undertaken on all assignments and tests. The internal verifier will also convene and chair the standarization meetings held at least twice a term.
- Standarization meetings will involve all assessors on the programme, will meet at least twice each term and deal with randomly selected examples of assessed work – between three and nine complete portfolios of work undertaken since the last standarization meeting.
- Internal verifier's role at this meeting is to select the sample for review, distribute the sample for consideration and produce a final report on the work reviewed.
- Internal verifier produces a record of outcomes from the standarization meetings which will be available to the external verifier.

Sufficiency

- Internal verifier will establish common understanding of sufficiency of evidence for all outcomes and liaise with external verifier on this issue.
- Sufficiency issues relate to APL, in programme coursework and work-based evidence. If a dispute arises on this issue the internal verifier will arbitrate with parties in dispute.

Referrals/appeals

- In each case a second marker's views will be sought; if case continues the internal verifier will review procedures operated in each specific situation and where procedures did not appear to be correctly followed a reassessment will be suggested.
- Standardization meetings will review all referral/appeal cases to agree final decisions.
- Any candidate still seeking to appeal may involve the college's academic appeals procedure.

GNVQ is an assessment-led qualification which requires a change of culture from the previous delivery-led awards it replaces. Experiencing the development of their own portfolio of evidence for an assessor award is an important first step in this culture shift for a member of staff. Many staff have found it challenging but insightful, and a great asset in their ability to contemplate what form 'evidence' could take and the difficulty of managing a portfolio-building process. However, this experience in itself has not permanently changed behaviour – the ongoing reinforcement of an active and developmental internal verifier has far more impact on the culture shift, because this is a new role to most staff who are not used to being so accountable to their own colleagues for their assessment activities. Indeed, because it can be a challenging role to undertake the staff involved have asked for continuing support and development even after they achieve a D34 qualification. A college-wide structure for internal verification is an important support mechanism which the college is developing alongside a staff development programme for those involved. Moreover, a team approach to verification, in which the internal verifier manages a process involving all the delivery team has been accepted by staff as the easiest way to operate verification and develop the whole assessment programme simultaneously.

Commitment to Change

The agenda for the third year of GNVQ development at the college will focus on the establishment of open access support facilities for core-skill development. During the second year, programme team managers met regularly to review the implementation issues of GNVQ and to monitor the new mechanisms in place to support their students. One area which had not been addressed was the way in which the college as a whole, rather than a particular delivery team, could support the development of core skills. Sharing experience had proved that no team could agree how much support was needed for cohorts of students and that each of the eight vocational areas had remarkably different degrees of access to core-skill facilities and staff. The monthly programme managers' review meeting agreed that the college should develop open access facilities to support individual students' needs in any or all of the core skills, and that while vocational staff are still responsible for the assessment of core skills through their assignment work for mandatory and option units, core-skill teams will be established to provide in-depth learner support for those in need using a workshop-based approach. These teams will help the vocational staff to develop more assessment opportunities in their assignment programme and will provide a cross-college internal verifier for each core-skill area to ensure the achievement of more consistent standards of acceptable evidence within the college across all vocational areas.

After two years of development the commitment to working together across vocational boundaries to address implementation issues and create a consistent approach for the whole college has become firmly established. It has proved a supportive and creative experience for the staff involved and created a powerful forum in which to make decisions about programme design which could shape the college's development. The support of senior managers has enabled this cross-college forum to make an impact on the way the college has been restructured as well as what if offers the general public, because they have recognized the need to pursue the consequences of particular curriculum changes rather than isolate them and deny their potential strategic implications. Staff need that kind of commitment from their managers. Staff think and plan within the constraints imposed and maintained by the institution in which they work. Where managers at all levels can encourage their staff to feel that those constraints can be revised and removed, then more creative thinking can and will take place.

Figure 2.4 is the product of an exercise created during the college's in-house GNVQ staff development programme designed to illustrate the interdependence of staff planning and the institutional framework in which it takes place. By asking staff to examine any aspect of the college's operations – timetabling, resourcing, publicity or enrolment for example – and place it on any of the bands illustrated in Figure 2.4, they soon perceive a pattern of implicit characteristics which affect their own planning. Asking them to reverse this process and design delivery from the other end of the continuum has radical implications for the way the institution

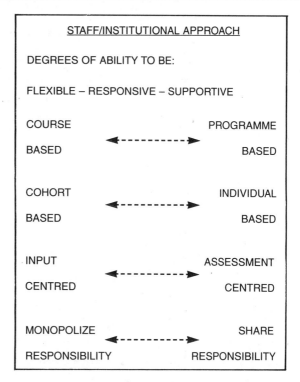

Figure 2.4   Staff institutional approach – the need for change.

needs to approach the organization of provision. This exercise is also useful in separating individual beliefs and actions from collective practice. For example, most staff do display great responsiveness towards individual learners on their programmes and will argue that they are flexible deliverers. However, the programmes they plan are rigid administrative monoliths which conform to, as they see it, the control requirements of their managers.

As Figure 2.4 indicates, the ability of staff or the college to be flexible depends on the degree to which their thinking, planning and delivery is cohort-based or individualized. As the GNVQ is a sophisticated design there is also a need to recognize the spread of responsibility for advice, guidance and support for the learner; it will not come from the delivery team in isolation. Indeed, these issues arise in describing a quality GNVQ provision. Figure 2.5 sets out what this centre concluded was a GNVQ Quality Checklist.

This checklist covers six interrelated areas, all of which are essential to effective provision. The three GNVQ levels of provision should be designed coherently – they are not isolated qualifications for they have an overlapping relationship which must be recognized in the planning stages, on implementation, and by the marketing function when presenting them to the public. This relationship

---

GNVQ QUALITY CHECKLIST

COHERENT PORTFOLIO OFFER

- range of levels designed sympathetically
- rationalisation of related programmes
- access to an identified wide range of additionals

THOROUGH INITIAL ASSESSMENT PROCESS

- action planning starts at interview
- screening for learner support
- identification of prior achievement to be accredited (imported)

STRONG PERSONAL MENTOR SYSTEM

- periodic/regular individual action planning/review
- well developed referral network for a range of support and additions
- continuous monitoring of progress/tracking

GOOD LINKS WITH INDUSTRY

- access placements
- assignments
- collaboration with key employers on GNVQ content/additionals

GOOD LINKS WITH SCHOOLS & HE

- liaison with Key Stage 4 work and compacts on entry/APA
- appropriate study skill development
- collaboration with HE on GNVQ content/additionals

EXTENSIVE STAFF DEVELOPMENT

- strong induction to GNVQ philosophy and technology of team and managers
- effective networking internally and externally
- comprehensive programme of assessor and verifier development well defined personal tutor training

Figure 2.5   GNVQ quality checklist.

between the levels is most evident at the initial assessment phase. For all candidates GNVQ can be presented as a four-year programme which can be entered in Years 1, 2 or 3 depending on prior attainment and need. Also, as an individual programme, learner support and the ultimate shape of their programme will be tailored to need not to a stereotyped or fixed provision. To make such a system work and achieve credibility a well-developed tutor network should be present to provide learners with strong support on-programme, with good industry and HE links to ensure good advice and guidance with regards to progression needs. All this must be

underpinned by senior management commitment to a clear rationale as to the role and purpose of GNVQ within the institution and
the local community it serves, and staff must be adequately supported to achieve that purpose.

The experience of GNVQ at the college has been a very positive
one of curriculum development which has led to considerable rede-
velopment of the college as a whole. Such change needs to be seen as
a three- to five-year programme which is not confined to one particular part of aspect of the college's work. Incorporation has taught us
that any one part of the institution depends upon all the other parts
working sympathetically. When a major curriculum change is introduced, as GNVQ was seen to be from the start, then all parts of the
college will gradually be affected and it is the management's
responsibility to review the operation of its parts and ensure that
the implications of change are identified and followed through to
create a dynamic and responsive environment.

NOTES

1. BTEC, *BTEC GNVQ's: A Guide for Centres*, October 1992.
2. NCVQ, *GNVQ Information Note 2:* Update of 14 December 1992.
3. For a more extended discussion of the impact of GNVQ curriculum
    changes see M. Horner and A.S. Lau-Walker, 'Staff Development for
    GNVQs' in *Journal of the National Association of Staff Development*, No.
    29, June 1993.
4. Grading has begun to be seen as a long-term problem for GNVQ – the
    University of London's Institute of Education concluded in its *GNVQ
    Assessment Review Project*, published in May 1994 that 'the current
    grading system for GNVQs . . . need[s] major reconceptualisation and
    reform and not simply fine-tuning' (p.1).
5. Taken from Judith Compton's presentation of initial findings of the GATE
    survey of access to HE, at Network Training's conference 'GNVQs and
    Access to Higher Education', 17 June 1994.

Chapter 3

TERRY COWHAM
AND ANNE BOURNER

Structure and Chaos: Introducing GNVQs as a Vehicle for Institutional Change

Background and Context

The announcement of the proposal to introduce a General National Vocational Qualification in the White Paper *Education & Training for the 21st Century*, coincided with Manchester College of Arts and Technology's (MANCAT's) need to search for a sense of order, identity and cohesion following chaotic reorganization of further education in Manchester in 1990. It is difficult to assess how much this local need in the 1990s sprang from and mirrored a national need in vocational education, which had been gestating over a longer time-scale through the 1980s.

Certainly the potential of a qualification which offered the benefits of:

1. a clear, coherent and flexible structure and framework focused on curriculum progression;
2. a student-centred approach to vocational education which embraced most of the principles which were being promoted through TVEI; and
3. a curriculum-centred approach to quality assurance,

seemed to present an opportunity for harnessing and promoting change at an institutional level, which made all the attendant risks of piloting and venturing into the unknown worth taking. While being conscious that GNVQ represented compromise and a hasty 'fix' by Central Government in an attempt to bridge the widening chasm between myopic academic and occupational training ideologies, the fact that it appeared to cohere with an emerging national curriculum structure and clearly indicated that important lessons had been learned from the mistakes made with occupational NVQs provided some underwriting of the risk.

Serendipity came into play when the labyrinthine process of searching for pilot status led to the college working with the RSA Examinations Board, who offered a refreshingly efficient, open, positive, supportive and consultative approach to centres undertaking the initiative.

Preparing for Introduction

Although a theoretical curriculum model had been prepared for the college with a view to pursuing quality and flexibility (see Figure 3.1), on which GNVQ could be superimposed as a formal structure, little ownership or understanding of this model had been developed across the college at course team level. The major issue in undertaking piloting at MANCAT was to effectively sell the initiative to staff and through them to students within a very short time-scale. A cross-college steering group was formed, chaired by the Vice-Principal responsible for Curriculum and Quality. Two other members from the College Senior Management Team, each responsible for managing a campus, were joined by two TVEI co-ordinators. It was decided to pilot on two of the college's three campuses which had been part of different institutions with very different cultures until 1990, but not at the central campus. The TVEI co-ordinators were to undertake GNVQ centre co-ordinator roles, operating at a campus level.

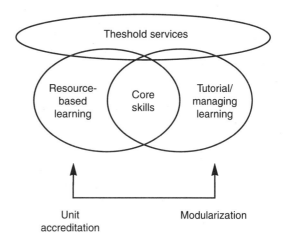

Figure 3.1 Curriculum model for MANCAT.

A key principle adopted from the outset was that staff development would be conducted on a cross-college basis, involving all the programme teams which, it was proposed, would pilot GNVQ (i.e. the five phase 1 programme areas). Again serendipity came into play in that the first staff development seminar uncovered a very powerful model for development. It was decided in haste and with little opportunity for reflection that the first seminar should consist of:

(a) a key note presentation introducing the structure and principles of GNVQ along with the case for undertaking a pilot with RSA;
(b) staff working in programme teams to address the practical issues of introducing GNVQs through mapping GNVQ against existing curriculum offerings as well as conducting a needs analysis. A Steering Group member joined and worked with each team. Heads of Department who had elected to attend also joined a programme team from their department;
(c) each programme team being asked to feed back on their proposals, problems and needs (i.e. proposed Action Plans).

This approach which focused on team-work, involving consultation and sharing of knowledge and experience by all present, provided a rich and positive experience for all concerned. The richness of the cross-fertilization generated by teams from disparate curriculum areas and cultures, working in close proximity and sharing their proposals, plans and experiences with their peers, cannot be over-stated. Needless to say this was a generic model for staff development that was adopted and developed for all future events.

Among the needs that were identified and addressed were:

(a) an allocation of £5,000 for GNVQ from the soon-to-disappear GEST budget, with £1,250 being held centrally and £750 being allocated to each programme team contingent on the submission of a reasoned justification;
(b) the establishment of resource files on GNVQ for programme teams, provided by Centre Co-ordinators;
(c) the design and production of a standard MANCAT GNVQ Student Portfolio;
(d) an immediate need to plan and provide further staff development seminars on core-skill mapping and on assessment.

It was interesting in the context of MANCAT that, although from the outset a strong commitment was given to institutional development, co-ordination and planning, each of the five phase 1 programme areas produced different development needs, problems and approaches which were explored and developed within the overall framework and which each contributed to institutional development and understanding.

The first year of delivery

Inevitably the hasty introduction of GNVQs, which manifested itself particularly in the last minute and late publication of the standards, many of which were inappropriate in content and written in incomprehensible language, meant that staff were placed under great pressure and had to rely heavily on their experience of delivering student-centred vocational education. Core skills proved to be particularly troublesome, with some of the numeracy standards being felt to be unreasonable for Art and Design and Business Studies in particular, yet inadequate to the needs of Manufacturing. Information Technology required considerable staff development in some areas where particular problems of embedding the standards were experienced by programme areas unused to using IT.

The commitment to staff that the college would produce a student logbook incorporating an action plan and the standards for each GNVQ programme placed a heavy load on the Centre Co-ordinators. NCVQ assisted in this development by copying the standards onto disk which assisted in desktop publishing and word processing of the logbook, which were issued to all students by the October half-term. Subsequently the 'MANCAT Logbook' has been approved by External Verifiers from all three awarding bodies as the basis for the student portfolio of evidence. Part of the logbook is reproduced in Figure 3.2.

It had been impossible to anticipate the amount of evaluation which was to take place and which began four weeks into the programme. To quote one of our co-ordinators:

> Every agency in the world descended on the Phase 1 Centres and took samples of everything they could lay their hands on, asked millions of questions and took up valuable teaching and learning time. Students began to wear a hunted look and ran from anyone dressed in a suit and carrying a briefcase. Consultants and academics, including a myriad of teachers undertaking M.Eds on GNVQ, took to courting staff delivering GNVQ in an attempt to find some examples of students' work.

However, there were many positive aspects to be gained from the level of national interest in the development. From the first staff development event we had decided to 'celebrate' the college's involvement in the introduction of GNVQ. A certain excitement was engendered by programme teams as they derived the curriculum and delivered it from a set of standards. The opportunity to revise and update teaching methods proved to be a great motivating factor. The morale of staff and students was raised by the interest in their work and visits by staff from NCVQ, FEU and other agencies,

An Introduction to your GNVQ Log Book

MANCHESTER College of Arts and Technology

This log book is an important document used to record your success throughout your course. It is the way that you prove that you can understand and do the things listed as elements and performance criteria.

This log book contains:

- this introduction
- an action plan
- review sheets
- the three core skills units (pink, green and blue)

- the mandatory units (yellow/gold)
- optional units
- additional units (if used)
- grading criteria

Action Plan

This is a summary of the things you need to do in order to achieve success in your course. You will discuss this with your tutor so that action points can be agreed for the first tutorial. You can plan out your work so it fits your ambitions.

Review Sheets

These are to record your discussions in tutorials and to agree on the immediate actions you will need to take before the next tutorial. You are required to sign these to indicate that you agree with the course of action.

Core Skills

These are a range of skills that are not specific to any one particular course, subject or job. They cover a set of basic skills in communications, application of number and information technology and are common to all GNVQ courses. You will not be awarded the qualification if you cannot produce evidence to show that you have achieved in the core skills.

Mandatory Units

These are the backbone of the course. They are the units that are assessed by nationally set tests. All examinations boards have the same mandatory units and everyone doing a GNVQ in the same vocational area as you must have completed these units no matter how specialist the other units are. You will complete 3 at Foundation Level (level 1), 4 at Intermediate (level 2) or 8 at Advanced Level (level 3).

Optional Units

These are specialist units offered by the college from a selection written by the various examination boards. They may give your qualification a specific vocational direction. You will complete 3 at Foundation Level (level 1), 2 at Intermediate Level (level 2) or 4 a Advanced Level (level 3).

Additional Units

These are not compulsory, but may be recommended for entry to certain jobs or Higher Education. The number depends on the course and your final goal. They are specialist units.

Using the Log Book to Record Your Achievements

Throughout your course you will be taking part in a wide range of learning activities; completing assignments which may include practical work, visiting places relevant to your course, maybe undertaking work experience. All of these types of learning will help you towards developing the range of skills and knowledge listed in your log book. You will find that these are split into units, elements and performance criteria. When you feel that you have achieved all the parts of the element you may claim them. You do this by writing in the space provided where and how you have demonstrated your success in a particular activity. You are simply providing evidence of your success. e.g.

Assignment 3 – Design a Chair, drawings to design specifications, see page 7 of portfolio. When your tutor (assessor) signs the page after you have achieved the element, they are basically supporting your claim. The recording of evidence is your responsibility, if you do not complete this as you go along you may find it impossible to fill it all in at the end of the unit.

Grades

When you have completed all the elements of the course you will be awarded an overall grade. You have to show that in 33% of your evidence you can fulfil the criteria such as planning your work, sorting out the right information and you will be awarded a pass, merit or distinction.

You can always ask your tutor to explain any of the elements or performance criteria either in class or at a tutorial.

Figure 3.2(a) MANCAT log book: An introduction to your GNVQ log book.

Date:	Names:

Outline of learning programme with proposed completion dates:

Areas for additional work:

Short and long-term career goals:

Personal goals:

Figure 3.2(b) MANCAT log book: action plan.

REVIEW

MANCHESTER
College of Arts and Technology

Date:

Review number:

Signatures:

Discussion points

Agreed action

Figure 3.2(c) MANCAT log book: review.

Core Skills

Information technology level 3

Element 3.1: Set system options, set up storage systems and input information

Manchester
College of
Arts and
Technology

Evidence and Location

Performance criteria:

1. Information is entered in full and conforms to requirements / conventions regarding labelling, format and place within file(s) / record(s)

2. Information is entered using a format which will enable any subsequent editing to be carried out efficiently

3. Copies of drafts / source information are retained as directed

4. The organisation of storage system allows applications to run efficiently and allows efficient location, retrieval and transfer of information

5. Security routines are used to protect information from accidental deletion / disruption and tampering

6. Changes in system options result in faster, easier working

7. Changes in system options do not interfere adversely with other users' requirements

Range:

Type of information: textual; graphical; numerical

Type of application: those used for storing and presenting textual information; those used for storing and presenting graphical information;those used for storing and presenting numerical information

Storage systems: existing systems; new systems established by the individual (eg. directory systems, folder / file systems)

Labelling conventions: existing; new conventions established by the individual (eg. file names, directory names, information tags)

Type of system options: facilities relating to the working environment (eg. mouse speed, cursor speed, screen colours); initiating communicatouns between devices (eg. setting up ports, selecting and loading printer drivers)

Completed to Required Standard: Assessor Signature .... Student Signature .... Date: /   /

Figure 3.2(d)   MANCAT log book: core skills. Information technology level 3.

Core Skills
Information technology level 3
Element 3.2: Edit, organise and integrate complex information from different sources

Manchester
College of
Arts and
Technology

Evidence and Location

Performance criteria:

1. Correct information is retrieved using retrieval routines efficiently
2. Information is protected from accidental deletion/disruption and tampering
3. Unwanted information is removed and backup routines are implemented correctly
4. Editing/search/calculation routines minimise the number of steps/stages needed
5. Editing/moving/copying routines minimise risks of deleting/disrupting information
6. Information is saved/arranged in a form which makes it most amenable to transfer
7. Any discrepancies between the source material and new files/records are corrected if necessary

Range:

Type of information: complex textual information (e.g. report with a number of chapters and subsections); complex graphical information (e.g. illustrations, charts); complex numerical information (e.g tables of figures in column format)

Type of application: those used for storing and presenting textual information; those used for storing and presenting graphical information; those used for storing and presenting numerical information

Retrieval routines: word/character search, search for tagged information (e.g. file type, codes, labels), page finder (e.g. in applications for storing and presenting textual information), cell finder (e.g. in applications which manage tables figures, in applications which manage records containing textual information

Type of routines: search routines given to and identified by the individual (e.g. to search through textual records); calculation routines given to and identified by the individual (e.g. to work with numerical information); moving and copying information within and between files; using tabulation and indents; transfer of information between different applications

Completed to Required Standard: Assessor Signature ....   Student Signature ....   Date: /   /

Figure 3.2(d) *contd*

Core Skills
Information technology level 3
Element 3.3: Select and use formats for presenting complex information

Manchester
College of
Arts and
Technology

Evidence and Location

Performance criteria:

1. Final version of information is legible, accurate and complete
2. Output/final presentation corresponds with requirements
3. Waste is minimised during production of hard copy
4. Format options are used to create a format which displays information effectively
5. Format of the final version of information combined form different sources is coherent/consistent

Range:

Type of information: complex textual information (e.g. report with a number of chapters an subsections), complex graphical information (e.g illustrations , charts); complex numerical information (e.g. tables of figures in column format)

Type of application: those used for storing and presenting textual information; those used for storing and presenting graphical information; those used for storing and presenting numerical information

Type of output/final presentation: screen displays; hard copy

Choice of format: precise format parameters/commands given to the individual; format parameters/commands selected by the individual

Type of format: continuous prose; letters; labels; diagrams; tables

Format options: margins, justification; character set and size; portrait layout, landscape layout; page size; column text and figures

Information from different sources: information which must be combined from a number of source files and which requires a consistent format (e.g. indexing, section and page numbering)

Completed to Required Standard: Assessor Signature .... Student Signature .... Date: /   /

Figure 3.2(d) *contd*

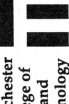

Core Skills
Information technology level 3
Element 3.4: Evaluate features and facilities of applications already available in the setting

Performance criteria:

1. The importance of accuracy and precision when using information technology (IT) is explained

2. The importance of using procedures which protect information form accidental deletion, disruption and tampering is explained

3. The ways that features of applications affect the efficiency of day-to-day working are described and evaluated

4. Facilities offered by applications which improve day-to-day working are evaluated, selected and used

5. Facilities offered by applications are used when they can improve day-to-day working in comparison with non- IT means of information handling

Range:

Choice of applications: the person uses given applications specified by those supervising the activity, the person can select and use facilities within given applications; the person can select and use facilities within selected applications

Applications: those used for storing, working with and presenting textual information; those used for storing, working with and presenting graphical information; those used for storing, working with and presenting numerical information

Procedures which protect information: security routines (e.g. passwords, file access labels), backup procedures

Effects on efficiency: positive, negative

Improvements in day-to-day working: Saving time, reducing cost, increasing efficiency, improving accuracy

Evidence and Location

Completed to Required Standard: Assessor Signature ....   Student Signature ....   Date: / /

Figure 3.2(d) *contd*

Core Skills
Information technology level 3
Element 3.5: Deal with errors and faults at level 3

**Manchester
College of
Arts and
Technology**

Performance criteria:

1. Information technology equipment is used in accordance with health and safety requirements

2. Errors and faults are correctly identified and prompt action taken to rectify them

3. Errors and faults which fall outside own scope are referred to appropriate personnel promptly

4. Approaches used to rectify faults and errors do not cause harm to persons nor damage to equipment and stored information

5. Prompt action is taken to alert others to the knock-on effect of identified errors and faults on their activities

Range:

Health and safety requirements: seating, lighting, screen orientation, arrangement of cables and work surfaces; avoidance of electrical hazard, avoidance of contamination/damage to equipment and media

Operations: setting system options, setting up storage systems and inputting information; editing, organising and integrating complex information from different sources; selecting and using formats for presenting complex information

Evidence and Location

Completed to Required Standard: Assessor Signature ....   Student Signature ....   Date: /   /

Figure 3.2(d) *contd*

including Higher Education Institutions. A consistent message which was received from external agencies was the positive approach and attitude taken by our staff to this development. Involvement in two FEU projects, one involving staff from Business Studies, Art and Design and Manufacturing in materials development, provided a positive boost to the self-esteem of staff and an increased confidence in their professional capability. Involvement in delivering staff development presentations and seminars provided similar benefits, and a wide range and large number of staff were used in this capacity, which served to further enhance the team spirit of GNVQ staff. An extract from a presentation made by one of the Centre Co-ordinators is shown in Figure 3.3.

OUTCOMES OF CROSS-COLLEGE STAFF DEVELOPMENT

These have been *practical* ('Getting the show on the road in time') and *psychological* (ownership, involvement, support).

OUTCOMES

We are now *specifically* familiar with:
- what GNVQ is
- what staff need to learn
- what students need to know
- what delivery changes are needed
- what learning activities are appropriate
- how assessment can be carried out and recorded
- how core skills can be covered.

We have also *more generally:*
- pooled problems and solutions
- shared encouragement and enthusiasm
- avoided duplication of effort through sharing good practice
- taken ownership of the programmes
- felt involved in the initiative
- thought hard about the curriculum
- addressed student needs with renewed attention.

Figure 3.3   Outcomes of cross-college staff development.

An early issue which arose in discussions with NCVQ and local HEIs was the availability of Additional Units to augment student programmes. Discussions were held with the RSA which resulted in a contract being lodged with the college for developing 30 Additional Units – six for each of the five phase 1 programme areas. In the event unit writing provided an extremely strong vehicle for staff development, as well as providing a platform for engaging the interest and involvement of local HEIs in GNVQ development.

Towards the end of 1993 staff development events in the college focused on developing a generic delivery model for GNVQ. It was agreed to attempt to introduce a modular structure with 'short fat' modules which would be completed in less than a term. The structure is represented diagrammatically in Figure 3.4. This structure

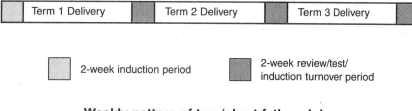

Yearly pattern of nine-week turnaround of modules

Term 1 Delivery	Term 2 Delivery	Term 3 Delivery

2-week induction period

2-week review/test/ induction turnover period

Weekly pattern of two 'short fat' modules

MON Module 1	TUES Tutorial	WED Module 2	THUR Additional studies	FRI Work experience

Figure 3.4   Pattern of modules.

was to be tried and tested during the second year of GNVQ, which would also see the introduction of three new programme areas and the level 1 Foundation GNVQ.

Piloting GNVQ Foundation

From the beginning MANCAT expressed great interest in the development of the level 1 Foundation programme and were involved in the FEU and NCVQ consultation. The introduction was planned to build on the experience gained from the Diploma of Vocational Education which was to be replaced at the Moston campus. The potential for providing progression opportunities for students who have achieved little at school, often with resulting disaffection, was the major factor. However, it was also becoming clear that the Intermediate GNVQ (level 2) was proving too demanding for students in the lower half of the cohort previously served by BTEC First programmes, and that opportunities were available for unit accreditation for school link programmes, which anticipated Dearing's report, and also for some students with special learning difficulties and disabilities.

The lessons learnt from adopting a corporate and collegiate approach to GNVQ programmes in the previous year proved to be particularly appropriate to Foundation. An integrated programme was adopted to enable the widest range of vocational options to students, thus preserving the opportunity for students to experience 'vocational tasters' as well as building a vocational foundation. At the heart of the programme, a core-skills stem based on tutorial support was developed. This enables students to develop and accredit their skills in core disciplines while developing vocational experience and aptitudes. This approach is expressed in Figure 3.5.

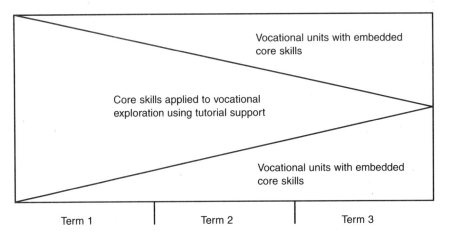

Vocational units with embedded core skills

Core skills applied to vocational exploration using tutorial support

Vocational units with embedded core skills

Term 1   Term 2   Term 3

Figure 3.5 Integrated structure for foundation programme.

A particularly important issue in delivering Foundation programmes proved to be the critical issue of providing learning support. Experience has demonstrated the importance of involving learning support staff in the co-ordination of the programme and in the core delivery team.

Experience was also gained of providing a link programme to a local school for a Foundation programme. The following conditions need to apply within the school if links are to be effective:

1. All members of the teaching team should have copies of all the documentation, including those relating to finance.
2. A clear contract of commitment from both sides.
3. A curriculum map and suitable assignment/learning activities drafted early in the partnership. This would cover the whole school curriculum not just GNVQ.
4. A timetable for the year should be produced. This should show the activities for the entire student cohort and identify the staff involved and their responsibilities.
5. Staff development of all Senior Teachers at the school.
6. Staff development of teaching team to D32/33 of the TDLB standards.
7. Staff development of Programme Co-ordinator to D34 of the TDLB standards.

8.   The minutes of all meetings to be circulated to all teaching team members and senior members of staff as communication is vital in an endeavour of this kind.
9.   Strategies for aiding the students to achieve across the range should be discussed before the programme starts and resources for supporting this process should be made available.

GNVQ Overseas

Early in 1994 various colleges were invited to tender for a project involving the introduction of GNVQs in the Sultanate of Oman. MANCAT, in partnership with RSA, were successful in having their tender accepted. A team of three staff began the process of introduction during June, based at the Muscat Technical and Industrial College. The first phase of introduction has involved:

1.   Preparing for Centre approval.
2.   Building TDLB portfolios for staff in Oman.
3.   Designing a one-year introductory programme for students, with a strong emphasis on English as a Second Language and Core Skills accreditation, which prepares students for GNVQ in learning experiences, terminology and procedures for recording of evidence and assessment.
4.   Developing college-wide processes for staff and curriculum development for:
     (a)   record-keeping systems;
     (b)   document control and standards for learning material development, production and dissemination in order to build a Curriculum Resource Bank;
     (c)   the development and operation of Learning Resource Centres;
     (d)   the design and development of student learning activities.

Most of these issues will apply to all prospective centres planning the introduction of GNVQ. A range of practical issues are identified in the next section, which complement the above issues.

Some Key points and thoughts from the 'chalk-face'

Learning activities and curriculum mapping

In most institutions a form of the 'bingo sheet' is used. This has all the standards down one side (y axis) and all the prescribed learning activities across the top (x axis). The holes in the grid are filled with crosses where the prescribed learning activity generates evidence to achieve the standard. In order to fill in a bingo sheet the programme team should pool all their previous work on the subject and see what can be recycled/updated and what needs to be generated in order to complete the bingo sheet. Many of the schools embarking on GNVQ have found their biggest difficulty is in producing learning activities because they often have no prior experience of the subject area.

It is useful to establish a 'house style' for assignments so that the entire programme team can take responsibility for an assignment and cover for each other if necessary. Information technology skills are useful for this.

One of the criticisms of GNVQ is that most evidence indicators ask for 'report'. A report can be anything from a video to a computer printout. It does not have to be a long essay. Variety in the forms of evidence presented makes a programme much more interesting for staff and students. Experience has shown that a video of any student activity is extremely useful for verification procedures as it is a useful reminder of the group members and their performance levels.

It is most important to include industrial simulation, industrial visits and if possible work experience in the programme as these can provide excellent evidence in the form of diaries or evaluations and it provides the students with career ideas and markets the course to local employers. If any of these methods are going to be used, it is vital that they should appear on the curriculum map to avoid duplication of subject areas.

The student brief for a learning activity must make clear exactly what the student must do in order to claim specified elements. In some programmes the tasks may be negotiated with the student and constitute a part of the action planning process. In other programmes there is a need to be more directive as the evidence is based on particular information sources or practical skills. The learning activities need to be flexible enough to cover a wide range of student abilities and must provide an opportunity for the student to achieve the grading criteria.

Core-skill integration

In schools and in some colleges there has been a movement towards establishing a group of specialist core-skills tutors. This does not work with GNVQ as the core skills have to be assessed as part of the vocational units. This has not been popular with some tutors as it makes them examine more closely what they are teaching and how core skills are part of that teaching. It has also highlighted the needs of certain staff to acquire core skills to an appropriate level.

A certain amount of innovation is needed by staff to identify the core skills implicit in their learning activities and in some cases to examine core skills to see how the higher levels of these can be included in learning activities. Again a bingo sheet can be used to identify which core skills are assessed in which learning activities.

Induction

Curriculum teams felt that there were three areas of knowledge needed by students during the induction period. These were as follows:

- college-specific information;
- department/campus-specific information;
- programme-specific information.

Any induction should be an active process wherever possible, any evidence generated during the induction period should be accredited. By writing induction learning activities that were programme-specific, the student generated evidence and underwent a diagnostic testing period in a painless manner.

Accordingly, Business Studies on the central campus successfully followed this schedule. Six weeks into term students were allocated to Intermediate and Advanced levels according to their performance. This has been a successful model because of the strength of the long-established course team and their commitment to the process.

Action planning

An action plan puts the student in control of his or her own learning. It is a vital part of the GNVQ programme as it evidences the grading criteria. Without any action planning it is very difficult for a student to give proof of achievement above a pass.

Basically an action plan is a method of establishing why and how the student is hoping to complete the programme and therefore the ways in which the tutor can aid her/him to achieve this goal.

An action plan is also a way of helping the student to face up to the realities of their performance by asking them specific questions and waiting for them to answer them. For example:

- What do you want to do as a career?
- What qualifications do you need to get a job in that field?
- What qualifications have you already got?
- What constraints (domestic, academic, time-scale) are there that might prevent you achieving this goal?

- What areas of study do you find difficult?
- What are you going to do about this?
- What areas of study do you find interesting/easy?
- Why do you think this is the case?

These are the kind of questions that can be used in a *Programme Action Plan* completed at enrolment or induction. The students will write the answers to these types of questions as their Action Plan. The tutor is there as navigator and adviser. The action plan belongs to the student and is a confidential document. It should be in their own handwriting or word-processed by them and signed and dated by the tutor and the student.

The Programme Action Plan is *reviewed* in one-to-one sessions during the course of the programme. The following questions may be asked at this type of session:

- Which assignments have you handed in?
- What is missing?
- What is a reasonable time-scale for completion of this work in time for verification?
- Which areas of the work do you find difficult?
- How are you (the student) going to deal with this problem?
- Why do you not turn up for certain unit classes?
- What are your plans for producing evidence for the next unit?
- You missed the last assignment, how are you going to provide evidence for that element?

Generally speaking the broad areas of discussion at a *review session* will be the same for all programme members and may be introduced in a group session. Individual sessions should take place privately so that the student feels relaxed enough to give accurate and honest information. Review session sheets should be signed and dated by student and tutor.

In order to achieve grades a student needs to provide evidence that they can plan, review and evaluate their own performance. One of the ways of producing this is through a *Learning Activity Action Plan*. Sometimes the form that a piece of evidence is going to take is decided by the tutor, sometimes by the student. The Learning Activity Action Plan can be a negotiating tool used either in a group session or in a private review session.

Different programmes in MANCAT have used different types of Action Plan; essentially the system of recording is not important, the majority of Action Plans have the same features. The process of listening and negotiating with the student is the important part.

In effect the action planning and tutorial processes together act as a formative Record of Achievement. If these documents, along with the logbook and student evidence, are kept together in the portfolio then student records are kept to a minimum.

The Advice and Guidance Service use action planning as a way of focusing students to the right course and as a way of giving career guidance when they are on the course.

Getting an Action Plan out of a student is a challenge! It requires persistence, listening skills and a strong stomach.

The student experience

GNVQ students have an overview of the vocational area, are able to find and organize information to suit their needs, have practical knowledge of the industry and are advocates for their own learning. Each GNVQ student has a portfolio that contains the evidence of their achievement, not the usual teacher-led statements that are sometimes encountered on Records of Achievement, but hard evidence of work done in the subject.

GNVQ students can work independently, are able to communicate, are numerate and can use Information Technology applications such as word processing, databases, spreadsheets and graphics. Their knowledge is not confined to the narrow remits of an occupational area but covers the entire vocational field. This means that they are more confident when discussing what they have learnt and are a useful marketing tool for the institution they have attended. They are advocates for their own learning. This contrasts with students who have followed a teacher-led qualification, who often do not have the same skills, and because they have been passive learners they are often passive at interview.

Postscript

The introduction of GNVQ, while providing the potential for chaos, has also provided the opportunity for structuring the college curriculum. Building on the experiences of piloting has provided the basis for a programme of unitizing the whole of MANCAT's curriculum with a view to providing greatly increased flexibility and enhanced quality. The college strategic plan now identifies the development of a curriculum model for the college, which will reflect a GNVQ core integrated with NVQ Additional Units, which is intended will reflect and develop a European model for vocational education and training. This is represented in Figure 3.6.

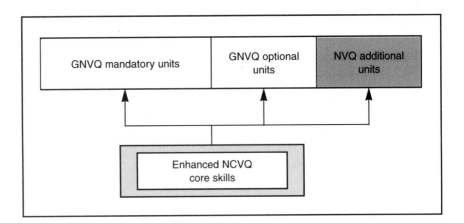

Figure 3.6 Proposed core curriculum structure.

PART TWO Implementing Vocational Study
Through GNVQs

Chapter 4

SYLVIA WILLERTON # GNVQ in Art and Design

Prior to starting the new GNVQ qualifications in September of 1992, when we had been accepted as a pilot school, we realized that a great deal of planning and resourcing would have to be done to try to give ourselves the best chance of successfully operating such a new concept in Art and Design education.

The establishment is a large 11–19 comprehensive school in Wiltshire with a good reputation for its educational standards and above average A-level examination results. It has always seen vocational education as an important strand in maintaining diversification and choice for its students, having been involved in CPVE and DOVE courses from their respective inceptions. This background, stretching back many years, was to prove invaluable experience in setting up and organizing the GNVQ.

Having attended numerous meetings and taken part in wide-ranging discussions we tentatively set about writing assignments for all units at Intermediate and Advanced levels. Our policy was then, and still is now, to write some assignments which are unit-specific and some (in fact, the majority) which are holistic in nature embracing many of the performance criteria and range from different units. Although this needs extremely careful monitoring and recording it is far more akin to a natural and progressive art and design process than, for example, individually isolating Unit 1; Two-dimensional visual language and Unit 3; Three-dimensional visual language from Unit 6; Working to art briefs, or Unit 7; Working to design briefs from Unit 8; Evaluate and present work, etc. Because of our strongly held belief that core-skills units *had* to be an *integrated* part of the course, it was also decided at that time, and still continues today, to incorporate them into all assignment writing and to teach them in the faculty area. Some expertise is needed in various aspects of core skills but this has been achieved with the co-operation and direction from teachers in other faculties.

One of the chief considerations that had to be contemplated was that of time. A great deal of time is needed for students to be able to complete the courses. Our experience has shown that around 18 hours at least are needed for the Intermediate course and around 22 hours for the Advanced course. This can be achieved in many ways; we, in our establishment, have adopted the following in our time management:

1. Providing a studio for the exclusive use of sixth-form Art and Design students, which is available for student's unsupervised use at any time. This allows them space of their own in which they can leave materials, etc., and gives them the opportunity to continue their work independently.

2. Sixth-form students have an afternoon each week of Complementary Studies when they can choose from a comprehensive list of cultural, aesthetic, sporting or personal skill-based activities. GNVQ students are strongly recommended to enhance their experiences and to incorporate some of the activities into their GNVQ assignments. For example, a silversmith and an expert in copper-beating were brought in for a series of ten-week courses, and photography is on offer – along with courses in batik, enamelled jewellery, weaving and creative textiles.

3. The student's Industrial Placement was carefully considered and prepared with the object of placing students in Art and Design based industries, as were compiling and writing questionnaires with regard to business practice, health and safety, etc., so that information could be gathered which would form the basis of parts of the Business and Professional Practice unit or practical work which would enhance their coursework.

4. Industrial Tutors are a regular feature of the sixth-form timetable. Management personnel from local businesses work with small groups of students conducting discussions about how companies, and the world of work in general, operate.

5. We have a variety of sixth-form activities in which students are expected to participate and organize themselves, and which we have successfully combined into GNVQ students' experience and domain: activities like the school production (last year it was the musical *Grease*) where assignments were built around set design and poster/ticket/programme design; The Charity Challenge, a large-scale fund-raising activity involving the whole of Year 12 for which a group of GNVQ Art and Design

students designed and printed T-shirts, painted a mural and made a large piece of ceramic sculpture which is now on permanent public display as a commemoration of the event; and the town's annual carnival which provides GNVQ students with the opportunity of designing and building a float for the Carnival Parade. These assignments are treated seriously and are fully developed using action planning, research and development and are critically evaluated and recorded in appropriate forms. Much of this work is completed in students' own time: the work for *Grease*, the Charity Challenge and the local carnival had to be.

6. Many students supplement their GNVQ work by opting to take a GCSE in an allied subject; ceramics is popular, as are graphics and design technology. Assignments are set in these subject areas which are modified to suit both aspects of the respective course.

7. In Year 13 the GNVQ Advanced-level students are given a whole day each week out of school when they are expected to pursue GNVQ activities such as a weekly work-experience placement, visits to museums, galleries, etc., researching assignment topics or simply getting on with their work at home or in the studio.

Contact time (i.e. timetabled time with a specialist tutor) is approximately 11 hours for Intermediate students and 14 hours for Advanced students. The rest of the time is made up by the use of all the above-mentioned policies with access to the Art and Design faculty equipment and/or space and to staff for impromptu advice when possible, and a lot of time spent on homework.

The first year

Initially we decided to put all our GNVQ students on to the Intermediate course (then called 'level 2'). This was done so that we could see how the course developed and that, irrespective of the students' option for staying either one or two years in the sixth form, we, and they, would hopefully have achieved some success after one year.

There was at this time a view held in the centre by some non-GNVQ staff and students that this course was for the less able student and that it was going to be 'an easy option'. Probably this was a legacy left over from previous vocational education courses. It has taken some time before the realization has dawned that here is a course that demands a lot more work and student commitment, and the standard and workload of level 3 (now Advanced level) are much more akin to traditional A levels.

We had one student who had completed one year in the sixth form doing two A levels and who was about to drop out of school because her interest had waned and she could not cope. It was suggested to her that here was a new qualification and that she might consider having a go at it. After much deliberation and discussion we decided that she would attempt level 3 (now Advanced) GNVQ in one year. She had already completed one year of A-level Textiles (and had completed a work placement in the textile business) and this she would continue as she would be able to use that work as part of her GNVQ work. This meant that effectively she would be a full-time Art and Design student at school. Work was set for her to start during the summer holiday in 1992 – work which concentrated mainly on drawing skills, observation and visual language. This gained that bit of extra time we knew she would need if she was to complete two years' work in one year. She knew from the outset that if she was going to succeed she would have to be fully committed and have to make an extraordinary effort to complete all of the assignments for the mandatory and optional units and successfully take every test. In the first year tests for the mandatory units were all short-answer papers, and were very unsatisfactory as many questions were inappropriate or set to the wrong level.

This student took to the new course like a duck to water and was a changed character within a very short space of time. She became more confident, started to enjoy what she was doing and began to see the point of what she was trying to achieve and the direction in which she was aiming. Her parents also noted a much more positive attitude at home.

On the other hand, however, some parents were confused. We had held meetings in school for them where the GNVQ was explained and then re-clarified as the course commenced, but remarks and comments in the media served only to confuse and undermine their confidence. It took a lot of good public relations tactics to restore confidence. One of the ways in which this was done was to mount exhibitions of GNVQ work, from all the subject areas, at regular intervals. This, along with the unmistakable increase in commitment and self-confidence of the students, quickly restored parents' confidence in what we were doing.

As the course began to unfold what was noticeable was the rise in the standard of the work coming from all students. This really was conspicuous and we put it down to their own commitment, the ownership that the work gave them and the enjoyment of being able to use a wide variety of resources, materials, techniques and processes. (We try as much as possible to give them practical experience of the whole range not just knowledge of the range.) Also, as the work began to develop away from the protected art studios and into the school and community where they had to stand on their own feet and be answerable to real clients and customers, their confidence was further boosted as they achieved success and were praised for their work.

Being a phase 1 centre, the school was inundated with visitors who, more often than not wanted to talk to students about their work and the course. Consequently students had to talk to Inspectors and officers from OFSTED, the Department of Employment, NCVQ, City & Guilds, lecturers from colleges and teachers from other schools, and the Minister for Higher Education. After their initial nervousness the students became quite articulate and were comfortable in talking about and explaining their work. They took it as a matter of course that if a visitor came into the faculty they would explain what they were doing; in fact by the end of the first year if a visitor didn't talk to them they felt quite put out!

It became quite apparent both to ourselves and to the students that during the first year most of them were going to want to continue into the second year of the sixth form and were voicing their intention to move on to Advanced level GNVQ. They were enjoying the course and they were beginning to produce work which was within the performance criteria and range of Advanced GNVQ. Some of this was due in part to the one Advanced-level student previously mentioned. Her commitment and enthusiasm were rubbing off onto the others. In the end, with only one exception, all the students opted to stay on for the second year and all moved on to take the Advanced level.

This commitment and enthusiasm made it difficult to distinguish between the students on the GNVQ course and those taking the traditional A-level and the Modular A-level Art and Design examinations. One of the more noticeable distinctions was that the GNVQ students, on the whole, were the more articulate ones.

Three or four of the traditional A-level students (i.e. those who wished to pursue a career in Art and Design), having seen the range and scope of the work being produced by the GNVQ students, asked if they could join the course. They liked the way the course operated, the linking to business, the industrial placement, working independently, coming in to the studios at any time, etc.

So about three-quarters of the way through the first year we had:

- GNVQ Intermediate students who had become so keen that they were already committing themselves to staying on and doing GNVQ Advanced;
- one GNVQ Advanced student who was trying to achieve the award in a single year;
- A-level students who had started off on the traditional A-level course who had joined the GNVQ Advanced level course.

One problem that now began to arise was that of entry into higher education. Although we as staff realized that this was a genuine qualification which should have a lot of currency there was the nagging doubt about how higher education would see it. Would it be wholeheartedly accepted? Would the qualification be on UCAS and ADAR forms? When confirmation came that it would be accepted and it would appear on UCAS and ADAR forms it made our job much easier and we could feel more confident in advising students.

The greatest problem from the students' point of view was the record-keeping: the log books! They enjoyed doing the work; they enjoyed the visits; they enjoyed the group work and their own ownership of their work; they enjoyed compiling a portfolio of work, even the writing of evaluations; but they found the filling in of the log books in such a meticulous way, making sure that performance criteria and the range were correctly identified tedious. This made a lot more work for us as staff, as we had to do a lot of chasing-up to ensure that it had been done properly.

This particular problem has become easier as time has progressed. New cohorts of students realize that it has to be done. Word of mouth from student to student is an effective communicator. One of the points that we will no doubt reiterate would be that log books should be completed and kept up-to-date at all times. As each assignment is completed then the performance criteria and range used should be recorded. It is essential therefore that staff familiarize themselves with the elements, PCs and range for all units as advice will need to be given to students at varying times throughout the course.

One way we have found useful is that at the end of some assignments students are asked to put up an exhibition of their work (see Figure 4.1). They have to show their Action Plans, the written brief, development of ideas using either roughs, workbooks, sketch-books, maquettes, models, etc., trials and evaluations, the finished work or works and *their completed log book*. They have then to talk about their work to staff, peers, clients (simulated or real) and an inspection of the log book becomes an integral part of the assessment. This

Figure 4.1(a)   Students displaying evidence of achievement.

Figure 4.1(b)   Students displaying evidence of achievement.

now poses no problems. They are happy to do this and are confident in their approach. Initially nervousness and accepting criticism did cause one or two students to worry, but when they saw that everyone had to go through the same procedure they were reassured.

The tests, which have to be taken for each mandatory unit, have developed over the two years of the course and no doubt will continue to develop further as the GNVQ itself develops. During the first year the tests were short-answer papers: approximately 30 questions had to be answered in one hour. They really were quite inappropriate and were either so all-embracing as to be too easy or so specific that many students didn't complete as wide an area as was expected. Some students had to sit several papers more than once in order to be accredited with a particular unit. This put undue pressure on them, and us, and was one of the most unsatisfactory aspects of the first year.

The second year brought about an improvement. The number of units to be tested was reduced, the historical context unit was omitted from testing. The papers were multi-choice answers, and the criticisms that had been levelled at the previous year's papers had been noted. The questions were directed much more to the range in each unit and were much more concerned with the knowledge that students should have acquired in completing the work.

One of our students in this cohort was dyslexic which meant that she had great difficulty reading the words and the questions. To overcome this we compiled a glossary of terms which covered every word we could find from the performance criteria and the range in all the units with which we thought she might have difficulty. This proved to be of interest to other students and so it was made into a booklet and produced for all GNVQ Art and Design students. They have all said how useful it was in preparing them for the tests, especially when user-unfriendly language appeared on the test paper; they now felt much more comfortable with their understanding of questions. The student with dyslexia was in fact bright and talented, her work was lively and imaginative and she completed the course with the award of distinction so her dyslexia did not prove to be an insurmountable problem.

It has to be said, however, that there is still widespread dissatisfaction with this method of testing Art and Design work, and that a practical form of testing may be more appropriate.

At the end of the first year all the students taking the Intermediate level, with the exception of one student who dropped out of school towards the end of the year, were awarded the qualification – some with merit and distinction at Intermediate level. The student who attempted the Advanced level in one year was also awarded the qualification with distinction. She thus became the first person nationally to achieve an A-level GNVQ and went on to a place in higher education on a BSc course in textiles.

The result of this was that, as mentioned previously, all the Intermediate students went on to do a second year and moved up to take the Advanced course. The Year 11 students coming in to the sixth form, having seen the work that was being produced and the style of the course, knew what they wanted and most opted to go straight onto the Advanced course. In fact, some students who started to work on the Intermediate course in 1993 did so well with their coursework and passed the first two tests straight away that they changed to the Advanced course.

The course was widely advertised in school prior to September 1993 and was offered as a separate option from traditional A levels. Thus, some of the students who would normally have been expected to choose three traditional A levels chose instead to take the Advanced GNVQ with one other traditional A level. Most of these students were those who wanted to pursue a career in Art and Design and had chosen an allied traditional A level to go with their GNVQ. In one or two cases this was the traditional A-level Art course, which effectively gave them a full Art and Design timetable. This was done after careful consideration and discussion as to their individual aspirations between student, careers officers, parents and teaching staff. Other students have chosen a contrasting traditional A level to go with their Art and Design GNVQ to give a broader base or to keep their options open. Certainly the status of the Advanced GNVQ has reached parity with traditional A levels in many students' eyes. They are fully aware of what they are letting themselves in for with regard to commitment and workload but can see the worth, the style and meaning of the GNVQ course.

We set assignments which are usually open-ended, and which allow students to use a wide variety of media, materials and processes in both two and three dimensions, and in both art and design contexts. Then a one-to-one relationship is built up with each individual student working independently on different assignments and at different speeds. This is a very demanding process on staff, much more so than any traditional teaching method, but this is a method that we have built up over a number of years using various modular courses. This individual approach and attention is the one thing that ensures that all students feel that they are in control of what they are doing. They know that they will stand or fall by their own decisions and, because their work is unique and their results are unlike anyone else's, that they cannot be compared with anyone else. Therefore whatever they produce will be a reflection of their own abilities, their own initiative and their own self-organization. These latter two are, of course, among some of the criteria used in differentiating and assessing pass, merit and distinction levels.

Figure 4.1(c) Students displaying evidence of achievement.

The addition of core skills has been a positive move. Whereas before Application of Number, Communication and Information Technology have been there in Art and Design, most students did not recognize: (a) the significance and importance of them in the Art and Design process, or (b) the fact that they were using them frequently without knowing it.

The core skill of Application of Number is used especially in design processes. Area, volume, size, the calculations for amounts needed, pricing and costing jobs, measuring scaling, etc., these are all part and parcel of Art and Design processes and should be seen to be so. Communication as a core skill has always been used – one has only to look at the sketch books of Leonardo da Vinci to see the copious notes made in his own individual style to realize this. Most artists and designers make notes in this way. Making sketches and drawing diagrams are forms of visual communication and are all part of a naturally occurring process. Information Technology is no problem for the majority of students, who are usually reasonably proficient in the use of computers and word processors. Our chief problem in this area has been getting sufficient resources to provide enough computers for the Art Department so that we can be independent and integrate this particular core skill without students having to wait until they can use the network of computers in the main body of the school.

The other area which was new to us was, of course, the introduction of a business element to Art and Design teaching. We had experience of putting students into work experience before and therefore we looked at that first of all. We again try to incorporate an understanding of business practice in all the assignments that we set, some are easier to incorporate than others. It is easy to work business practice into 'Working with design briefs' and into 'Work with technology', not quite so easy to try to fit it into 'Historical and contextual references'. As part of some of the assignments we have set up mini-companies which a group of students administer themselves. This has meant that they have had to assign positions in their company for chair, accountant, company secretary, etc. and as accurately as possible keep the books straight and, if possible, make a profit. A fridge-magnet production company is one example and T-shirt designs another. Above all we were, and are, determined not to use any 'bolt on' exercises for core skills or for 'Business and professional practice' – they *have* to be integrated into the work. This gives the course coherence and makes the whole process meaningful from the students' point of view. If students had to go to the Maths Faculty for Application of Number lessons, for example, they would not bring back with them the significance and understanding that the artist needs to have to fully appreciate the creative process.

Towards the end of the course students began applying for higher and further education courses through UCAS and ADAR and some for Foundation Courses in Art and Design. A few students were disappointed when some Higher Education Institutions demanded a foundation course as an entry qualification before looking at the quality of the portfolio. Hopefully this attitude will change as the range and depth of the GNVQ Advanced level are more universally understood.

Summary

Working with the specifications

All our assignment writing was based on the premise that core skills and vocational aspects of the course should be integrated. Assignments were written (a) holistically covering several units and (b) unit specific. The majority were written holistically but some, where we wanted to draw particular attention to some definitive learning outcome, were specific to that topic.

Planning and delivery issues

The initial planning had to be done a long way in advance of September 1992, but at that time changes were constantly being made and therefore we had to be flexible and try out several ideas to see if they would work.

Students were started on assignments which were open-ended enough to allow them the scope for individual development. They were required to write their own brief from the guidelines given; prepare an Action Plan; develop a sequence of ideas using as wide a variety of methods, materials and processes as possible; and evaluate the work, cost it and produce finished pieces, adding a summative evaluation to the whole which would be presented in either a portfolio or as an exhibition. This exhibition covered the presentation aspects in the mandatory units.

Other aspects that needed planning were time, finances and resources and expertise.

Sufficient time on the timetable is essential. In our experience Intermediate students need, as a minimum, about 18 hours per week on their work; 11 or 12 of these should be the minimum staff contact time. Advanced students need to spend a minimum of 22 hours per week on their work, 14 or 15 of which should be staff contact time.

In the initial stages extra finances should be sought. There is need for a wide variety of resources, computers, extra equipment, a reasonable choice of crafts as well as an extended range of traditional drawing, painting and three-dimensional equipment. It is impossible to build it all up at once but it is best to realize that, from the start, an ongoing process of adding resources has to be undertaken.

Expertise will need to be developed in those areas that are new. For example, the teaching and integration of core skills, expertise in Art and Design business organization and operation will have to be bought in or learnt by existing staff; new crafts and an understanding of computers and computer programs will also need to be utilized.

Student experience

Most students enjoyed the breadth and range of the course along with the independence and the ownership of their work which it gave them. They liked going out of school and finding real assignments that they could undertake. The linking of work experience and work placements with their GNVQ work was greatly appreciated. They also liked the fact that they could come into the department and work at their own pace in the studio provided. This despite the fact that there is a lot of pressure on them due to the sheer volume of work needed to complete the course. The result of all of this from our point of view was that there was a vast amount of work produced, a wide variety of topics tackled, and a large range of techniques, crafts, materials, etc. used in its production.

Tutor experience

We were extremely pleased with the attitude of the students and with their own self-generated motivation. We also found the quality of the work to be exciting and different because of the range that was presented to us.

We felt very pressurized, principally because of time. There never seemed to be enough of it and, during the first year especially, we had to put in a lot of extra time: lunch times, after school, even weekends, to make sure everything was completed. We felt an obligation to do this as this was the first year of a new course and we did not want any of the students to be disadvantaged simply because they were first-phase students. This problem has eased during the second year but it is still an issue.

Looking back and looking forward

One problem which occurred in the first year was with recording work in the log books There was a lot of work involved in this, especially when it got nearer to verification time and hours had to be spent by students and staff in getting them up-to-date at an already very exacting time. We have certainly learnt from this experience and log books are now being filled in as each assignment is completed. We are in the process of devising a method whereby students will be able to fill them in accurately and with confidence without (hopefully) needing to refer to a tutor.

We realize that, as numbers of students opting for GNVQ grows – and it has significantly grown each year – that more staff will be needed. In our faculty two more members of the Art and Design staff are being introduced to GNVQ teaching this year (1994/95). This will further increase the expertise we can offer and make the course more diverse for the students.

Finally, it is worth mentioning that a lot of the students who have successfully completed two years of GNVQ, both as Intermediate and Advanced students, are now going on to further and higher education into Foundation courses and BA courses. The majority of these students are those who would probably have left school at the end of Year 11 if this qualification had not been introduced. Two years ago they would not have believed that a further or higher education career was even a remote possibility for them. But they have been given this opportunity and have successfully taken it to achieve something real and positive. It is hoped that this will take them on to successful careers in art and design, which was always intended to be one of the aims of this new qualification.

The impact of GNVQs on Wootton Bassett Sixth Form

Wootton Bassett School is one of the largest comprehensive schools in Wiltshire. There are approximately 1,250 students aged between 11 and 19 enrolled. The site comprises 26.5 acres with accommodation based on several blocks. The campus contains a Youth and Community Centre and a Sports Centre.

The pupil population is truly comprehensive in nature featuring a range of abilities varying from potential Oxbridge university entrants to children with moderate learning difficulties in an integrated special unit. The sixth form was established in 1969. Since then the number of students in it has grown considerably and now approximately 250 students are housed in a purpose-built block.

In 1992 we were accepted by the City & Guilds of London Institute as a pilot centre for four GNVQ areas – Art and Design, Business, Health and Social Care, and Leisure and Tourism. (Science will be offered from September 1994.) This has made quite a significant impact on the social structure of the sixth form as well as on the option patterns of the timetable. Previously there had been a distinct, self-imposed division between the students on two-year

A-level courses and those on one-year vocational courses, even though they were based in mixed tutor groups. There appeared to be little contact between them and vocational students only frequented the Sixth Form Social Area on rare occasions. There was an undercurrent of lower esteem amongst vocational students. This started to improve to some extent in 1991 with the introduction of the Diploma of Vocational Education, but the various sixth-form committees that were elected by the students themselves were still made up entirely of A-level students.

A marked change in attitude was noticeable early in the first year of GNVQs and by the end of the first year the change was striking.

The new course had status. The fact that it was a completely new concept in education made students feel special. As a pilot centre we were host to a stream of visitors, many wishing to discuss the course with students. Self-esteem amongst the vocational students now grew considerably, they clearly became more articulate and took great pride in their work and in the course.

As some of the GNVQ Advanced students were also taking a traditional A level the divide between the academic and the vocational began to diminish. The sixth form began to be more unified. By the second year it was impossible to distinguish between the students on traditional A-level courses and those on vocational ones. Many GNVQ students, displaying organizational and management skills, were taking prominent roles in the sixth-form committees and in organizing activities for students in the lower age ranges of the school.

The staff involved in the implementation of the course worked extremely hard to 'get it right', holding regular meetings between the four areas which helped to give consistency and credibility. With this greater involvement of staff there were added constraints for the timetable (and still are) as most staff were not only involved with GNVQ work but needed to be used in their own faculties and with the other age ranges in the 11–19 band.

The choice of A-level courses on offer has always been wide-ranging, and the introduction of GNVQs has made the options patterns and subject combinations even wider (see Figures 4.2 and 4.3). As the school had a long-standing experience of both vocational and modular A-level programmes, the assimilation and delivery of the new GNVQ courses were not too difficult. During the first year approximately one-third of Year 12 had opted for vocational courses. The second year saw an increase to half of the new Year 12 cohort choosing GNVQ courses. As they progress into Year 13 in the coming year it is estimated that 50 per cent of the sixth form will be involved in GNVQ courses with an increasing number of students choosing an accompanying A or AS level. We advise against taking more than one A-level with GNVQ Advanced as the workload would be too great to do justice to each subject. Each student's timetable is negotiated to individual needs, interests and abilities.

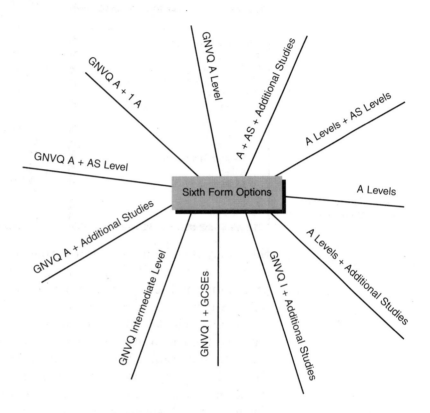

Figure 4.2 Possible combinations of courses available in Wootton Bassett Sixth Form.

A programme of Complementary Studies is part of the timetable for all sixth-form students. It is designed to provide balance in the curriculum and to broaden the interests and encourage the personal development of each student. One session a week (known as 'Forum') is devoted to a core programme which includes health education, political and moral understanding, study skills, environmental and community issues and careers advice. Representatives of various organizations are also invited in as guest speakers so that the opportunity is given to discuss major topics of interest.

In addition, as part of this Complementary Studies programme, Year 12 students enrol for three, ten-week modules (see Figure 4.4) which take place on one afternoon each week. Certificates are awarded to students who satisfactorily complete each course and

GNVQ Intermediate and Advanced.
Art & Design
Business
Health & Social Care
Leisure & Tourism
Science

Additional Studies
Accounting
FLAW (Foreign Language at Work) French/German
Sports Leadership Award (CCPR)
Word Processing
   GCSE
   Ceramics
   Child Care
   English
   Design Technology
   Italian
   Mathematics
   Spanish
   Travel & Tourism

A and AS Level
Art & Crafts
Biology
Business Studies
Chemistry
Computer Studies
Design Technology
Economics
English Literature
Further Mathematics
General Studies
Geography
Graphical Communication
History
Home Economics
Law
Mathematics
Modern Languages (French and German)
Music
Physics
Religious Studies
Textiles
Theatre Studies

Figure 4.3 Subject options available in Wootton Bassett Sixth Form.

these may then be used as part of their Record of Achievement. As students move into Year 13 they continue to participate in the core programme and some pursue a further programme which may lead to the A-level General Studies examination at the end of that year.

GNVQ students can make their choices to complement and enhance their own area of work. For example, Health and Social Care students could choose working with handicapped children at the hydrotherapy pool or first aid or even community service. Additional subjects (see Figure 4.3) can also be selected in this way. For example, Business, and Leisure and Tourism students are all encouraged to take FLAW (Foreign Language at Work) in French or German.

This is a bank of modules on offer as part of the Complementary Studies programme. The list is flexible and additions are added according to student demand.

Health-Related Fitness (YMCA Award)	Car Ownership	Enamelling/Copperwork
First Aid (St. John's Award)	Rugby	Golf
Trampolining	Carpentry	Silversmithing
Badminton	Photography	Geology
Word Processing	Swimming	Tennis
Hockey	Batik	D-I-Y
Hydrotherapy	Football	Squash
Self-Defence	Dance	Weight Training
Catering (Certificate in Health and Hygiene)	Community Service	Creative Textiles/Weaving

Figure 4.4 Complementary studies.

All sixth-form students work with Industrial Tutors from local firms who give advice on job applications, interview techniques, etc. Specialist advisers from a variety of professions also visit the school to hold group seminars with interested students. All these experiences have been utilized by GNVQ students and have become a successful part of their courses.

During their time in the sixth form all students have the opportunity to complete further work experience or a placement in industry. This is seen as an important and vital part of all GNVQ students' courses.

GNVQ students obviously spend much of their time in the vocational areas, but this is still a school situation and so they are expected to take a full and active part in sixth-form and school events and activities. What has been so successful over the last two years is the way they have incorporated all these activities into the GNVQ domain.

Chapter 5

NICK BAILEY GNVQ in Business

My sixth form college had experience of running vocational courses. As an 'open-access' sixth-form centre to our partner schools we had to be more than an exam factory providing HE fodder. The college has a well-established tradition of adding value to students who would have otherwise fallen out of mainstream education and drifted into employment or 'training' with little or no progression opportunity. To cater for this group of teenagers who are largely disaffected and usually demoralized, one-year GCSE retake courses were offered. Success in the one-year sixth guaranteed entry to a two-year sixth course and access to Further and Higher Education and enhanced employment prospects.

The one-year sixth was successful for students with some GCSE success (grades C–D but without the minimum of 4 Cs needed to enter a two-year course). For students with poor or no GCSE grades, the lowest quarter of the 'ability' range, the college could offer little. BTEC General had been tried and been successful but was replaced by CPVE which promised more variety, experience and choice for students, but as everyone now recognizes was aimed at too many goals to ever score for everyone. CPVE did provide courses but with no real demands on students and no reward that an employer or college would value. As a college we felt that this group of students was being poorly served and we looked at the courses which had been newly brought into the NVQ framework to provide a substantial course with recognized achievement.

The new BTEC First Diploma in Business and Finance (September 1991) was the preferred choice. This course was competence based, prior knowledge was not a major requirement, unlike a one-year GCSE retake course, and it offered two levels of attainment for students from the same course at NVQ levels 1 and 2, and we could offer a choice of routes through Administration, Finance, or Secretarial Skills. The course was successful, all students who completed received a recognized award and all had positive progression to either employment or NVQ level 3 or equivalent courses. The college, flushed with the success and the positive reaction of students and employers during work experiences, explored the expansion of vocational courses for 1992/93.

Our interest in vocational competence-based courses led to talks with the different awarding bodies about the proposed General National Vocational Qualifications. NCVQ asked us to participate in some research into core skills assessment and we were 'hooked'. The summer term of 1992 was spent preparing GNVQs in Business, Leisure and Tourism, and Health and Social Care. The college took the strategic decision to only offer GNVQs at level 2 during the pilot. We had no experience of vocational courses at level 3 and as a college we were very successful at A level and could see no reason to dilute that; we also had experience of competence-based learning at NVQ levels 1 and 2 not at level 3.

During the initial stages of preparation we also found NCVQ and the awarding bodies somewhat transient. Draft standards were late arriving, 'advice' was unreliable and often contradictory. The college decided to continue with the BTEC First Diploma in Business and Finance and to offer this in conjunction with GNVQ level 2 Business and GNVQ level 2 Leisure and Tourism. It was my job as co-ordinator to sort out how this could be done.

The solution to the problem was complex and in some ways worked very well. There were further constraints placed on the courses in that full staffing was not to be provided so that at times three courses would be taught simultaneously by one or two teachers in up to three locations.

The college insisted that work experience would be a component of the course for one day a week. This was a budget management not an educationally based decision and had been anticipated and argued against to no avail. It reduced students to a 0.8 timetable and excluded them from a lot of extracurricular college activities. We also knew from experience that one-day-a-week work placements were difficult to arrange and less effective than block placements. Few employers are willing to give a commitment for a whole academic year; most consider a term 'too long' and this results in students trying to arrange their own place and ending up working part-time for an employer they already work for, or a friend or member of their family, if they ever actually go to 'work experience'.

A further complication was added at this stage with the withdrawal of the BTEC First Diploma, which had been put into NVQ format, and its replacement with the new syllabus that closely followed the content but not the pattern of the GNVQ level 2 Business standard.

Also at this time senior management at the college took the decision to have the RSA as our awarding body for GNVQ rather than BTEC for whom we were already an approved centre. This added to our administration and resulted in entirely different and non-compatible documentation, procedures and even student recording. Naturally the decision was taken without consultation by the Vice-Principal, who was also centre co-ordinator, and not communicated to the teaching staff actually preparing the courses until some time later. This proved to be one of the themes of our GNVQ courses, the role of centre co-ordinator, and led to a lot of centre co-ordinator complaints. (And jokes such as: How many centre co-ordinators does it take to fix a light bulb? We don't know, they won't tell us.)

Given the limitations imposed by the college on the course and a mix of staff, some of whom were part-time and one instructor not a qualified teacher, I organized the courses. There were three steps taken. Firstly, a complete curriculum mapping exercise to identify all the required outcomes for each course. Secondly, a grouping together of the outcomes to identify commonality where possible across the three courses. Thirdly, a review of all assignments used and available within the Business Faculty of the college to see what could be used or adapted to meet the requirements and then identify what needed to be written. It was now possible to allocate people to courses and to give them preparation work.

One interesting result of the mapping exercise was the imbalance between the three courses in content and evidence requirements. The BTEC First Diploma in Business and Finance had the largest number of required outcomes and was subsequently timetabled across more blocks than the GNVQ level 2 courses. We justified this to students on the basis that the BTEC First had no examinations, but we remained mystified as to the actual reason since both courses were apparently of equal worth and standard. The GNVQ level 2 Leisure and Tourism had a significantly lower content than the level 2 Business. This was inexplicable and caused us some worry as to the relative merit of the Leisure and Tourism course. These doubts were raised at a meeting with NCVQ when the programmes were under way and only reflect the pilot programmes; the revised standards from September 1993 largely overcame these discrepancies.

The second major strategic decision taken was to teach the courses in an integrated way. This was partly because in order to match activities and outcomes we had to, and secondly because we felt easier with large integrated assignments that gave the students the opportunity to engage in broad investigations and realistic scenarios. We felt that many of the evidence requirements were similar and could be better met within a single assignment rather than having to revisit settings and concepts at different stages in the courses. It was an effective and time-efficient strategy and after discussions with centres that had adopted a linear approach who felt they were going round in circles at times rather than forwards, we felt relieved and justified. Our problems with the integrated approach came later in the course.

The course was structured with 12 hours per week timetabled contact for GNVQ plus a spare block for either a single GCSE in Mathematics, English Language, Geography or Human Biology; or students could follow the Youth Award Scheme at Gold Standard which represented core skills at level 2 in Communications, Application of Number, and Information Technology plus the Personal Effectiveness core skills not officially accredited by NCVQ at that time as units suitable for a GNVQ. Incidentally the BTEC students were fully timetabled on the First Diploma and had no opportunity to pursue a GCSE or other course at college. The remainder of all the students' timetable was filled with theology (compulsory for students, the one demand on them for attending a Catholic Sixth Form College), two non-examined liberal study courses, personal tutor time and some free-study periods. The pattern of the GNVQ timetable has changed significantly now partly due to the demands of GNVQ being recognized and partly to the exigencies of FEFC funding.

One of the problems with the GNVQ pilot year, 1992/93, was the lack of help and advice available. Between June 1992 and January 1993 we received no official help as a pilot centre and only had one preliminary visit by an external verifier and that was for Leisure and Tourism. The external verifier for Business was not appointed until 1993 and then came to us for advice. We felt very much in the dark and were convinced that along with a lot of other centres we must be reinventing wheels within wheels. Naturally we were.

The first confirmation that our courses were on line, and that as a centre we were broadly right in our approach to GNVQs, came from RSA course co-ordinator/internal verifier meetings that started in January 1993. This was the first time that information was not second-hand, was up-to-date and could be questioned. Liz Walters, head of the GNVQ Unit at the RSA, chaired the meetings. Key points raised at this stage were the basis of assessment, requirements for students completing Cumulative Assessment Records (CARs), core skills delivery and assessment, and how should moderation/internal verification work since many pilot centres had no source of comparison as they were running one programme with a small team. FE centres felt more confident as they usually offered the GNVQ parallel with a BTEC or similar course; schools were largely disadvantaged. At this stage of the pilot massive differences in the way courses were being resourced were becoming apparent, from the equivalent timetable of a single GCSE to over 20 hours fully staffed at level 2. At level 3 the diversity was less great, reflecting the established difference between a two-A-levels course in a school and a full-time vocational course in FE.

It became clear at this stage that most centres had opted for a linear delivery, working through the units in sequence and addressing each element – each performance criterion even – in turn. Some centres were trying to demonstrate each aspect of the range for an element against each performance criterion; they felt completely overwhelmed and had students repeating tasks and providing cabinets of additional material. Clarifications given at the co-ordinator/internal verifier meetings and the chance to discuss practice with other centres were invaluable. It was the hard practical advice that teachers delivering the courses needed, unlike the bland reference received from centre co-ordinators who in the most part were members of institutions' senior management teams and well removed from the presence or day-to-day needs of students. The involvement and commitment of senior management helped develop a wider curriculum but did very little in actually implementing it.

The integrated approach worked as far as we were concerned and allowed our bold attempt to merge courses, students, teaching and assignments. In the early stages of the course we could give all the students the same assignment, only needing to revise the topsheet to indicate what criteria and core skills, or common skills for BTEC, were to be demonstrated. Leisure and Tourism students needed their assignments flavouring to reflect the context and the needs of their range statements, but for marketing, promotion, record keeping and providing customer service they could follow the Business course. In fact the Business course provided more depth and breadth than the Leisure and Tourism standards. In the middle and later stages of the courses the paths parted as the common ground had been covered and each group had to concentrate on its own particular evidence. Leisure and Tourism only merged with Business for core-skill support in assignments, mainly IT. The BTEC First group continued working on similar assignments as GNVQ Business for half their timetable but, due to the greater volume and breadth of evidence required, they were taught separately for the remainder, followed different assignments and had to meet a far broader range of criteria in the common skills than the GNVQ students had in core skills.

The unit tests provided the first real barrier for GNVQ students. Originally in the pilot there were six mandatory units, all tested to show knowledge and understanding of the criteria and the range, with an 80 per cent pass mark. Unit tests had to be passed in order for the unit to be certificated, six certificated units plus core skills was a level 2 GNVQ. The results of the Business students were disappointing. As a result of the integrated approach, with assignment working rather than formal teaching, the underpinning knowledge required by the tests was not complete or was not recognized by the students in the test. The course team reviewed strategy and decided we had to teach to the test otherwise students were not going to get through the hurdle and their portfolio of evidence would be worthless without the corroborating unit test pass.

In the GNVQ level 2 pilot units the knowledge was organized in a somewhat arbitrary way. We had not recognized divisions of understanding and had got students to present evidence of their understanding and competence in a fully integrated way using large assignments, e.g. 'A New Business Proposal', which with tutoring the students could be steered to provide evidence covering many performance criteria from many elements and units across many ranges. We made some attempt to catalogue all the opportunities but with increasing diversity of the students' work we had to give up and put the onus on the students to record their individual achievement. Naturally the students did not recognize the specifics of the content of their course for two reasons. Firstly, we had 'translated' NCVQ-speak into student-friendly language for assignments and in our teaching. Secondly, the unit tests themselves were presented in a case study/data response format by the RSA which exceeded the reading skills expected of the students by core skills. In view of this and the 80 per cent pass mark there was little room for students to show their actual understanding if they had not fully understood the case scenario. Answers were not specified but produced by the student and were then subject to interpretation by the examiner.

Business students felt particularly let down by the tests. We had a poor pass rate, the tests were hard and even though the students tried and worked their coursework success was not confirmed. Leisure and Tourism students had an almost 100 per cent pass rate – even a student whose absenteeism was of legendary proportions, who had missed most of the teaching, passed all six unit tests at the first sitting.

We felt very let down by the whole testing issue in GNVQ. It defeated the whole point of the course in providing an alternative to the academic route based on competence and evidence of understanding. The GNVQ students would have to sit at least six hours of exams to gain the equivalent of four GCSEs, and possibly 12 or 20 hours until they were successful – far more than a student following a four or five GCSE course where course work could play a 100 per cent role and exam success or failure was not crucial to the final mark and achievement.

NCVQ heard the complaints from pilot centres and revised unit test success to four out of six. It was also 'confessed' that the addition of the unit test to GNVQs was a political decision imposed on NCVQ. The original intention had been a wholly evidenced award like the BTEC First or National. This did not help students succeed or motivate staff.

The external verification process proved to be the next hurdle. The external verifier for our Business programme was a 'late starter' and an independent consultant. Her experience of vocational education was limited. Initially we explained all about GNVQs, how we organized the course, our reasoning and strategy and course planning. In return we received nods of approval until we came to a final verification meeting where we hoped that a lot of students' units could be signed off and certificated. Instead we received our first advice. The students' CARs were inadequate, with not enough information about how students had met performance criteria or where that evidence could be found in their portfolios. We were devastated. We had assumed, like many centres, that CARs were simply a sort of register of completed work. Students filled them in when we told them a unit was finished, we signed it and it was filed in the portfolio. CARs, it now appeared, were to be a detailed account of how the performance criteria and range have been met and where exactly that evidence can be found by a detailed reference to a task or page of an assignment in a clearly indexed, ordered portfolio. We realized that students completing the assignments may only be half of the work of a GNVQ; students identifying how and where they met the requirements of their programme was the other half.

That verification occurred at the end of May and we had to disappoint plans for staff and students about the second half of the summer term in order to complete the course. Traditionally, one-year courses at the college finished with the Spring Bank Holiday; now they finish in July as a result of GNVQ. There were two clear benefits to this. Firstly, students who had completed all their work needed the time to put their portfolio and CARs in order. Secondly, some weaker students, who we thought would be unable to get a GNVQ in a college one-year course, now had the chance to complete and did so. (Some of those students are now following an Advanced level GNVQ: an important lesson for the college.)

During the Spring and Summer we received drafts of the proposed new standards after the advice and lessons from the pilot schemes had been accepted by NCVQ. There were significant changes at GNVQ level 2: a reduction from six to four mandatory units and the introduction of optional units that would not be tested. Eventually only three of the mandatory units were to be tested, Financial Transactions being the odd one out. The revised scheme was a major improvement on the pilot, offering choice and greater breadth and depth for students. The revised Leisure and Tourism scheme recti-fied a number of the discrepancies with Business but did not clear all the remaining doubts or criticisms. (At the time of writing, Leisure and Tourism is being reviewed by NCVQ and the awarding bodies at levels 2 and 3 in view of the persisting doubts as to its rigour and comparability with equivalent A levels or Advanced GNVQs. Revised standards should be available for implementation in September 1996.)

It was about this time that the Secretary of State made some important announcements about GNVQs and called them 'voca-tional A levels'. The full impact of his statement was to change the names of GNVQs to Foundation, Intermediate, and Advanced for levels 1, 2, and 3. The statement came in the summer term and caused a lot of confusion with the next cohort of students and their parents who had been to our open evenings and had heard all about levels 1, 2, and 3 but now thought that all GNVQs were Advanced level and wondered whether we were running the 'new' courses. The timing of the message left a lot to be desired and showed a poor understanding of education's annual cycle. It also followed the previous government announcement of A levels as the educational 'gold standard'.

After the experience of integrated delivery the courses offered from September 1993 would run in a linear fashion. Only the Intermediate GNVQ Business would be offered, no BTEC First.

Business and Leisure and Tourism would run as discrete courses. Assignments were written to provide assessment opportunities for specific performance criteria and with regard to the range statements. Student-negotiated activities and alternative work that did not meet the specification of the described activity would not be acceptable. Thus the content and standard of work would be more consistent and verifiable. Intermediate Business was organized on a mandatory units first basis to allow as many testing opportunities in the year as possible. Optional units would be available when the mandatory units were completed. The course would be tightly programmed with activities, visits, speakers, etc. planned and organized in advance and deadlines for all assignments identified for the whole course. This level of planning is absolutely essential in order to guarantee that students will have the chance to complete and that resources will be available when needed.

When the course started a regular weekly meeting was included on the delivery teams' timetables, though the actual meeting took place after the normal college day. Only half an hour was allowed though in reality meetings took an hour and never included any attempts to verify or moderate work but were simply used to discuss students, the current assignment, review weekly plan(s) and to look at the coming assignment(s), allocating work as need be. There were six members of staff on the team for two groups of 16 students. Assignment writing was shared. Inputs were given to both groups combined where accommodation allowed. Each teacher took responsibility for a given number of students, the number depending on the proportion of time they were timetabled for on the course. Each tutor was then responsible for assessing their students' work, giving tutorial feedback and overseeing the action-planning of their students. Standards of tutorial support varied depending on the commitment and other demands of the teacher. However, the quality of tutorial support is an essential factor in the success of individual students and is a major factor in their motivation and perceived progress.

The 1993/94 Intermediate GNVQ Business course was a significant improvement on the previous year's. Twenty-one students completed the course, nine left the course either to go into employment or to leave the college, one transferred to GCSEs, and one to Foundation GNVQ Business. We achieved 100 per cent success, with three distinctions, one merit and 18 passes. The student who transferred to Foundation GNVQ Business also passed.

Our first Advanced group was started in September 1993 after the pilot. This was a wise decision. The pilot was for one year; the

Advanced is a two-year course. Advanced students caught up in the pilot had to transfer to new standards, had the units altered, saw the guidelines change and the unit test pass mark reduced from 80 to 70 per cent. It must have been a slightly disorienting course. We learnt a lot from our experience of the level 2 pilot and from other centres who ran the level 3 pilot. We carefully planned the pattern of the course, allocated responsibilities amongst the course team for writing and preparation of material, and discussed, critically but constructively, everything we wanted to do. The plans worked but we are reviewing the approach adopted.

We decided to take a tightly programmed and highly structured route for the first year of Advanced GNVQ. This was because we are used to running courses that way with lesson-by-lesson planning for a term published for students. The programme leads the course, and staff and students work to it. With a teaching team it is highly effective as everyone knows exactly what they are going to be doing and when. With Advanced GNVQ Business it worked but with certain costs. All the teaching team had to be familiar with every piece of work and every unit, element, criterion, range, assignment and the weekly programme. This lack of specialism created a huge workload for everyone and resulted in the weekly 40-minute meeting being largely spent discussing the current assignment. Secondly, two members of staff took it upon themselves to do all the assessment and to give the tutorial feedback, the other three team members giving input and running workshops. This had the effect of only two team members being really aware of student performance and of building any individual rapport with students. These problems were recognized and dealt with; now all members of the Advanced team have an assessment and tutor role.

The one major criticism of using a highly structured approach to delivering a GNVQ is that the students can be denied the opportunity to demonstrate the grading criteria. The student can obtain a pass grade by undertaking every task, meeting all the deadlines and following the prescribed timetable and plan. The opportunities for any evidence of their own planning and information gathering are going to be very limited. They are precluded from claiming distinction since the student 'independently draws up plans of action for complex activities. The plans prioritise the different tasks within the given time period'.[1] Secondly, a highly structured approach does not teach the students how to plan, how to organize their work and define the priorities. The development of the students' personal effectiveness, which is what in essence the grading criteria measure, is limited. In order for a student to achieve a grading they have to have met the grading over at least 30 per cent of their portfolio. (The NCVQ booklet, *Grading Advanced GNVQs*, May 1994, gives a much clearer explanation of the requirements.) We have recognized that the students on the Advanced course are going to have to become a lot more self-reliant and unlearn the routine way of working to programme if they are going to evidence a merit or distinction award.

In defence of using a highly structured and programmed method of delivery however, it does guarantee the weaker student a clear opportunity to achieve the GNVQ. They only have to demonstrate the criteria from the standards, no demand is placed on them to demonstrate more complex skills in terms of conceiving their own work, interpreting criteria and identifying their own evidence. As long as students work consistently and methodically and meet the minimum standard for assessment they can achieve an Advanced GNVQ. They can have multiple opportunities to attempt unit tests until they are successful and can have work referred as many times and with as much advice as it takes until they produce a satisfactory demonstration of criteria that can be used as evidence. These students are the ones who have most to gain from GNVQs because it guarantees access to the Advanced level, with their achievement being equivalent to two A-level passes, something they probably would not gain with the increasing emphasis on academic success being measured by examination.

We joined the pilot Foundation Business GNVQ in September 1993. As this was the pilot and a lot of comment, criticism and review have taken place it is unfair to discuss what will probably be a one-off programme. One point about Foundation GNVQs in general however is this. They are aimed at exactly the same cohort of students as Intermediate GNVQs, i.e. 16-plus students with limited GCSE success. It is very difficult to tell a Foundation GNVQ student from an Intermediate GNVQ student when they register for the course. However a decision has to be made fairly early on as to which programme students are going to follow because the evidence required for each course, even in the same subject area, is different. It is not possible to teach Foundation and Intermediate students together, they require different input and have to produce different evidence. Where the evidence for Foundation is compatible with that of Intermediate it is scattered over many units, some of them options and results in a 'scatter-gun' approach to delivery which makes the production of CARs for the Foundation students very difficult. Besides, in our experience the only real indicator of likely future achievement of students in a GNVQ is their attitude. If they want to work, are determined and methodical, they can achieve

GNVQ success, though it may take a lot of intensive revision and preparation for unit tests. An able student without the organization and some tenacity does not stand a hope. Prior knowledge, which can produce some GCSE success, is almost irrelevant at GNVQ, it is the production of evidence that is paramount. The worst single thing about Foundation in the current format is that it demands that centres differentiate at an early stage of a one-year 16-plus course and then immediately denies a group the opportunity they anticipate.

The lessons learnt from the pilot year, together with the experience and improved rationale for organizing and co-ordinating the Intermediate and Advanced courses, paid significant dividends. In essence the factors that lead to success are strategic decisions, long-term planning, short-term planning, induction, co-ordination, assessment and verification. Each is discussed below.

Strategic Decisions

We made a number of decisions before we did anything else, based on the experience of the pilot year, and again after the experience of the new standards across all three levels. The decisions that we took were, firstly, to have a linear unit-by-unit pattern with clear deadlines for all assignments and a deadline date for referrals usually three teaching weeks from the end of the unit. Secondly, to fully integrate core-skills evidence within the vocational work portfolio. Therefore opportunities to demonstrate the appropriate criteria had to be planned and mapped across assignments. Thirdly, to deliver mandatory units first to allow weaker students more opportunity to retake unit tests as needed. Fourthly, to use block not one-day-a-week work experience and to identify the units when it would be most applicable. Finally, to decide on the order of units. We felt this was crucial at Advanced level since the first unit is Business in the UK Economy and is rather bookish, boring and daunting so we opted for the more interesting units to catch students' imagination and to give them some 'real' activities such as making a television commercial as part of Unit 3 Marketing and being interviewed by a major international company who were willing to participate as part of Unit 4 Human Resources.

Long-term Planning

We planned the whole course in advance for Intermediate and the first year for Advanced with a rough very flexible outline for the second year. We started with the college calendar to identify holidays, whole college activities, year group activities, etc. and allocated weeks to units then initial deadlines for assignments. We created buffer weeks to allow flexibility since we did not know the dates of the unit tests and needed to allow time for them and for revision activities. We planned the mandatory units first, allowing an average of five weeks (in practice they varied between three and seven weeks) each and planned for four weeks per optional unit. Core skills were also 'allocated' to assignments as more or less appropriate to keep them vocationally relevant and to avoid the 'bolt-on' activity some centres devise which leads to a 'Frankenstein's monster' situation from the students' point of view when it comes to compiling the portfolio and CARs.

Short-term Planning

Short-term planning involves day-by-day, lesson-by-lesson planning. The role of the course co-ordinator is to make sure it all happens. This needs two skills from the co-ordinator: firstly, an awareness of everything required by a unit – element, performance criteria, range and core skills – and when they are intended to occur in the course and whether it has already happened, whether it was satisfactory and whether students need further opportunity; secondly, communication within the delivery team. GNVQ has to be a team effort and successful teams need team members not individuals. The role of the weekly course meeting is to find and solve all the problems that can defeat the success of the course, make sure everyone is aware of the problems and how they are going to be solved, who is going to do what and when that is going to happen. If the communication is not adequate, and the team does not work effectively, the course will fall apart very quickly because the students recognize that things are not gelling. They receive contradictory advice or information, see different standards of assessment for the same work and lose faith.

Induction

A GNVQ course is unlike anything done by the student before (unless a student is progressing from one level to another, but that is, in the main, exceptional). There is a new philosophy students need to understand that is different to all the education they have received before. They are going to take far more responsibility for their own learning and achievement. They are going to plan their own activities within a framework and are going to be in control with staff there to assist them when they want, if they want. This is very different to the schooling that most will have received prior to the course and they need to learn the basic skills that will allow them to be successful. We also include an introduction to core skills and make sure that everyone has a minimum IT competence so that they can use the college's IT facilities. Students then have no excuse for not producing work in the manner specified if that is a required outcome. We provide all students with a standard double density 3.5-inch floppy disk that is compatible with all the computers available in the college, recognizing that IT is an essential and assessed part of their course. We have also used induction to over-come some of the more esoteric number requirements of core skills.

Co-ordination

At the planning stages regular meetings are important so that team members are aware of what is going to happen and what their contribution is likely to be, and to allocate assignment preparation. Once the course is running regular co-ordination is essential. We use a standing agenda for meetings (Individual Students, Assess-ment, Planning and Co-ordination, Any Other Business), keep the minutes on file and make a point of discussing positive student actions as well as negative ones. These minutes prove useful for corroborating any grading claims for students; they are used by staff when compiling evidence for their TDLB assessor awards, are useful to demonstrate various aspects of the course to the external verifier in the event of proof of course team action planning being needed, or to highlight points that it is felt should be mentioned in the external verifier's report. It is the job of the course co-ordinator to produce the minutes and circulate information required for meetings, follow up the action required and report back any matters of interest to the course team.

Assessment

We share assessment but always discuss what is to be acceptable for a particular task/assignment. General rules of thumb we use are:

1. If it is to be of publishable quality (i.e. a letter or report etc.) then the work should be complete and correct, word-processed, with no spelling errors and correctly laid out and presented. If it is only intended as evidencing students' understanding then it should be legible, complete and correct.

2. All tasks, activities and requirements of the assignment should be included, be completed and correct. Anything less is not acceptable.
3. All work should include a front-sheet stating what the work is, what unit, element and criteria are being demonstrated, and what is included in the work. Students consider this unnecessary at first but after explanation that in six months' time they may need to refer a total stranger to one piece of the assignment from amongst a portfolio of 20 or 30 assignments by providing a simple written reference rather than personally pointing the piece out, and that if the visitor cannot find the work easily the students will not get their GNVQ, then they get used to it and much better at it after they have had to produce their first CARs.
4. If the work is in any way not complete, is incorrect or the quality of presentation insufficient it is referred back to the student with a detailed explanation of what is required in order to make it satisfactory. The student also receives verbal guidance at their weekly feedback tutorial and a record of that is kept as part of the student's action planning.

Verification

We verify at two levels. Firstly, for each course, to make sure that assessment is consistent between assessors (the team members), by sampling each assessor's assessment and also by more formal moderation-type meetings where a range of work can be discussed. Secondly, at a college level when the internal verifiers (IVs) for each area – Art and Design, Business, Health and Social Care, Leisure and Tourism, and Science – compare examples of core skills and agree assessment guidelines. The centre co-ordinator is responsible for administering the IV meetings and publishing the decisions about standards and acceptability.

Conclusions

For us GNVQ has worked. We 'signed on' to the idea and agree wholeheartedly with the aims of the initiative. It has extended the number of students at all levels who can achieve and has provided progression to students who would have otherwise fallen out of (or been left out of) full-time education.

As a Business course GNVQ is very good. Business in any form of study is vocational. Business is about what people actually do, unlike Economics which might be about what they, firms or governments might do if . . . but then again . . . , or Sociology which is analytical, descriptive but not in any way, from the student's point of view, applied. Businesses affect every aspect of a student's life – employment, future employment, consumption, entertainment, the media – and is the one subject typical of our society, reinforcing the values and knowledge the student is surrounded by. Business and the related aspects of the subject are by far the largest single area of vocational study at all levels. It is not glamorous, creative or artistic but it does lead to real opportunities, it does open doors, and it does explain, to some extent, our world. The GNVQ Business courses recognize this and provide students with the knowledge and understanding to 'do' business. They acquire skills and become competent in a way that very few academic courses ever expect students to, and choice is increased as they progress. Employment or education? The choice does not have to be made between either with a GNVQ, but the opportunities in both are enhanced. GNVQ students do not become specialized but increase their scope, not diminishing the focus as is usual with academic progression.

In the next few years it would be interesting to see a comparison of views between traditional academic route students and GNVQ students as to how they see their future and what is available to them from their study. I know what mine would say, how about yours?

Notes

1. *Revised Criteria for Grading Foundation and Intermediate GNVQs.* London: National Council for Vocational Qualifications, 1994, p.16; *Revised Criteria for Grading Advanced GNVQs.* London: National Council for Vocational Qualifications, 1994, p.16.

Chapter 6

LINDA WYATT # GNVQ in Health and Social Care

Why GNVQ?

Ferndown Upper School is a co-educational, non-denominational comprehensive school on the outskirts of Bournemouth, close to the Dorset/Hampshire border. It caters for the educational needs of approximately 1,200 students aged 13–18 years. The school aims to provide its students with a secure framework within which their aptitudes and abilities can be fully developed in preparation for adult life.

The sixth form consists of Year 12 and Year 13 and is rapidly expanding. In 1991/92 the 246 students registered were able to follow a one- or two-year programme of study combining a variety of academic and vocational subjects. With the introduction of the City and Guilds Diploma of Vocational Education, academic studies could be complemented by vocational skills. My role within the sixth form was that of Diploma of Vocational Education Co-ordinator where I was responsible for all programmes of study taught on the Providing Health and Social Care section.

In February 1992, the school was approached by City and Guilds and asked if we would like to be involved in 'piloting' the General National Vocational Qualifications. The decision to accept the invitation to join the 'pilot' was not taken lightly. We saw the development of GNVQ as a positive step forward which would offer our students an alternative to A-level studies as well as offering the flexibility required for a growing sixth form which caters for all levels of ability.

Initially we were led to believe that GNVQ was an extension of the Diploma of Vocational Education and that is what we planned for. The timetable allowed for ten hours of teaching time, per fortnight, in each of the vocational areas we 'piloted': Business;

Health and Social Care; and Leisure and Tourism. Within this time we saw both the level 2 and level 3 students.

How did we progress?

We began to try to match the Preparatory Modules from the Diploma of Vocational Education with the GNVQ specifications, to no avail, and we soon began to realize that GNVQ was a completely new ball game. It was like entering a 'black hole', being faced with the unknown quantity, knowing we could not go back, only forward. At this point, we took the GNVQ specifications and began to work at understanding the requirements and how to implement programmes of study that students and staff could follow.

GNVQ Health and Social Care

In September 1992, GNVQ Health and Social Care was available at two levels: level 2 (Intermediate) and level 3 (Advanced). For the purposes of this case study the focus will be level 3 (Advanced) (see Figure 6.1). We had six students who began the programme, one of whom dropped out very early on, finding the course of no interest to her.

The Advanced Level consists of:

- Eight mandatory units of which seven are tested;
- Four optional units which vary between awarding bodies;
- Core skills of Communication, Application of Number and Information Technology to at least Level 3.

Figure 6.1   Advanced GNVQ content.

We produced a planner to include all the vocational units that a student had to complete in order to achieve full accreditation (see Figure 6.2). This provided a framework within which students were expected to work whilst still enabling them to achieve the grading themes. It was decided that two mandatory units should be achieved each term, plus one optional unit. Obviously, having lost one term with the initial problems we knew the programme had to continue to the end of the summer term, and realized this might present problems for students taking A-level examinations.

With time against us, the core skills were added to the units when appropriate and if any core skills were omitted it was decided that a 'mopping up' exercise at the end of the programme would be permissible.

Unit 5	Health promotion.
Unit 6	Structure and practices in health and social care.
Unit 3	Physical aspects of health.
Unit 8	Research in health and social care with Unit 1 Access, equal opportunities and client rights.
Unit 4	Psychological and social aspects of health and social care.
Unit 7	Care plans.
Unit 2	Interpersonal interaction.

Figure 6.2   Order of delivery for Vocational Units.

Health and Social Care introduces students to the knowledge and skills necessary for further study or employment within a health and social care context. Students are able to investigate the needs of different client groups: children, adolescents, adults and elders, and look at how these needs are currently met through the existing health and social care provision. Throughout their studies, students develop an awareness of health and social values based on:

- freedom from any type of discrimination;
- maintaining confidentiality of information;
- promoting and supporting individual rights and choices;
- supporting individuals through effective communication.

GNVQ is a very student-centred programme of study where students are encouraged to take responsibility for their own learning and assessment, but this can only be achieved gradually with support and guidance from staff. To assist in this, an Activity/ Assignment proforma was designed (see Figure 6.3) that would enable staff to 'drip-feed' the specifications to the students in manageable quantities as well as provide a means of documenting any core skills that were achieved through the work. This produced an 'in-house' style for all GNVQ areas and offered consistency and standardization across the school. Using this form of documentation required an overall sheet that charted a student's progress through the numerous activity/assignments, and so the Matrix sheet (see Figure 6.4) was devised. This has proved to be a valuable formative document for students, assessors, internal verifiers and external verifiers.

It is true to say that there are no shortcuts to success – anyone taking on the delivery of a vocational area *must* work through the specifications in a logical and organized sequence that suits the individual establishment within its locality. The problems we experienced in the 'pilot' days resulted in us closing ranks and

School Name		
Logo · GNVQ:		
Level:	Activity:	

BRIEF:
This is the EVIDENCE INDICATOR with additions to make as 'real' as possible for the students.

AIMS:
These are the ELEMENTS to be covered within the activity.

PLANNING SHEET
Plan of action

What information will be needed?	Where will it come from?

How will your evidence be presented?

VOCATIONAL OBJECTIVES

The PERFORMANCE CRITERIA is listed.	The RANGE relating to each PC is listed.	PAGE NUMBER	STUDENT SIGNS	ASSESSOR SIGNS

CORE SKILL OBJECTIVES

The RANGE is listed.	The PERORMANCE CRITERIA is listed.	PAGE NUMBER	STUDENT SIGNS	ASSESSOR SIGNS

GRADING LOG

The grading log is reproduced here for students and staff to monitor whether a
PASS
MERIT or
DISTINCTION
is being obtained.

EVALUATION OF THE ACTIVITY
Method of delivery

What I did?

What I learnt?

What would I change and why?

Record of teacher/tutor intervention.

Recommendations.

Assessor signature   Date

Student signature   Date

Figure 6.3   Activity/Assignment Proforma.

SCHOOL:		GNVQ RECORD SHEET:

STUDENT:	START DATE:
GNVQ AREA:	LEVEL: ADVANCED

UNITS	ELEMENTS	ASSIGNMENTS/ACTIVITIES																								UNIT TESTS		
		1	2	3	4	5	6	7	8	9	10	11	12	13	14	15	16	17	18	19	20	21	22	23	24	25	Gained	Date	Mark

MANDATORY VOCATIONAL UNITS

Unit	Element
1	1.1
	1.2
	1.3
2	2.1
	2.2
	2.3
3	3.1
	3.2
	3.3
4	4.1
	4.2
	4.3
5	5.1
	5.2
	5.3
6	6.1
	6.2
	6.3
7	7.1
	7.2
	7.3
8	8.1
	8.2
	8.3

OPTIONAL VOCATIONAL UNITS

Figure 6.4(a) GNVQ Record Sheet.

UNITS		ELEMENTS	ASSIGNMENTS/ACTIVITIES 1 2 3 4 5 6 7 8 9 10 11 12 13 14 15 16 17 18 19 20 21 22 23 24 25	KEY
CORE SKILLS	A	3.1		**A** Number
		3.2		
		3.3		
	B	3.1		**B** Commun-ication
		3.2		
		3.3		
		3.4		
	C	3.1		**C** Information technology
		3.2		
		3.3		
		3.4		
		3.5		
	D	3.1		**D** Problem solving
		3.2		
	E	3.1		**E** Working with others
		3.2		
	F	3.1		**F** Improve own learning and performance
		3.2		
GRADING		DRAW UP		
		MONITOR		
		IDENTIFYING & USING SOURCES		
		ESTABLISH VALIDITY		
		EVALUATION		
		JUSTIFICATION		

ASSESSOR:	COMPLETION DATE:	DESTINATION:
INTERNAL VERIFIER:		
EXTERNAL VERIFIER:		

Key for filling in grid on matrix above.

■ = Element completed

◣ = Element partially completed

M = Merit grade

D = Distinction grade

Figure 6.4(b)   GNVQ
Record Sheet (continued).

tackling the specifications literally, at the expense of working in partnership with local businesses and industry.

Final outcome

The students have been hard pressed to succeed in obtaining the full qualification, but this in no way affects their integrity and ability, neither of which has ever been in doubt. At the end of the first phase, Advanced Health and Social Care, only one student is likely to achieve the full award. The other four candidates have achieved six or seven of the mandatory units alongside two of the core-skill units. All these students were engaged in A-level studies as well as the vocational programme and, as anticipated at the beginning, it was difficult for them to return to these studies after their A-level examinations. On this occasion no student was penalized by being on the GNVQ programme as they did not need the full qualification for their progression. Their genuine disappointment is that they failed to complete all the units of work necessary for the full award – time just ran out! I personally would like to take the opportunity to express my thanks publicly to the students who took up the challenge of GNVQ during the 'pilot' years and hope that their portfolio of evidence will assist them in their future progression to:

- employment within a health and social care context;
- employment as a care assistant whilst studying to become a paramedic;
- University of Portsmouth Project 2000, Pre-Registry Midwifery Programme;
- Exeter, Tor and South West College of Health, Project 2000, Adult Branch;
- Luton University, BA Health Studies.

Combining vocational and core

Activity/assignment writing has relied on thorough understanding of the specifications. An example of how units can feed each other and provide a natural source of core-skill work is that of:

- Unit 1 Access, equal opportunities and client rights;
- Unit 8 Research in health and social care.

Recommendations from City and Guilds state: 'do not address too much in one activity because it will make gathering of evidence and recordkeeping too complex' (*GNVQ Handbook*, City and Guilds, 1993, p. 22). This is, in general, an excellent reminder, but by linking the two units together the students could use a variety of different teaching and learning styles in a very practical way. To avoid confusion we had to map out the necessary recording and monitoring in advance. Some very clear guidelines were set down and open discussions as a group provided the stimulus that enabled students to cover all the work in a co-operative manner without jeopardizing the need for students to have individual evidence for their portfolios. Figure 6.5 gives the wording of the brief.

'An investigation into the forms of research that are used in health and social care, giving advantages and disadvantages. Using these methods compare a number of experiences that demonstrate the impact of attitudes, social influences on behaviour, two forms of discrimination and their effects, and explain how legislation and systems assist in redressing discrimination and equal opportunities.'

Figure 6.5 The three R's: Research, rights and responsibilities.

The elements to be covered within this work included:

- 1.1 Investigate attitudes and other social influences on behaviour.
- 1.2 Investigate discrimination and its effects on individuals.
- 1.3 Describe how equal opportunities are maintained.
- 8.1 Investigate types of research used in health and social care.
- 8.2 Construct a structured research instrument to survey opinion.
- 8.3 Investigate methods of interpreting information.

During discussions the students decided on a general plan and then divided Unit 1.2 into sections using the 'bases of discrimination' range statement. Each group member would complete this element and Unit 1.3 using their particular discrimination and use this as the basis of research for Unit 8.1 and Unit 8.2. Students would then report back to the group to enable notes to be taken and questions asked. Unit 1.1 was to be completed by each member of the group as was Unit 8.3. The complexities of these activities gave enormous scope for the implementation of the grading themes.

Monitoring work

The need for student action plans is crucial to the success of such an enormous activity, as is the need for common deadlines for completion of Units 1.2 and 1.3 so that reporting back can occur without delay. Each student had a negotiated, signed assessment plan that highlighted the vocational and core skills to be covered, as well as the sources of evidence to be included.

Communication 3.1 Take part in discussions with a range of people on a range of matters.
Range: Audience – people familiar with the subject matter but not in frequent contact with the individual.
Covered in 1.3.
Communication 3.2 Prepare written material on a range of matters.
Range: Subject matters – routine matters.
Covered in 1.3.
Range: Subject matters – complex and non-routine matters.
Covered in 8.1.
Range: Format – freely structured documents.
Covered in 8.1.
Range: Conventions – use of full stop, comma, apostrophe, colon, capital letters, sentences, paragraphs, use of highlighting and indentation to enhance meaning.
Covered in 8.1.
Range: Audience – people familiar with the subject matter and in frequent contact with the individual.
Covered in 8.1.
Range: Audience – people familiar with the subject matter but not in frequent contact with the individual.
Covered in 1.3.
Communication 3.4 Read and respond to written material and images on a range of matters.
Range: Subject matters – complex and non routine matters.
Covered in 1.3.
Range: Format – pre-set formats.
Covered in 1.3.
Range: Format – freely structured.
Covered in 1.1.
Range: Images – used commonly in the context.
Covered in 1.1.
Range: Images – images which have been used by others to illustrate complex/difficult points.
Covered in 1.3.
Range: Sources of clarification – provided for the individual, having to be identified and sought out by the individual, written, oral.
Covered in 1.1.
Application of Number 3.1 Gather and process data at core skill level 3.
Range: Techniques – design and use an observation sheet to collect data.
Covered in 8.3.
Range: Techniques – design and use a questionnaire to survey opinion.
Covered in 8.2.
Range: Techniques – organize data into groups and classifications.
Covered in 8.3.
Information Technology 3.1 Set system options, set up storage systems and input information.
Range: Type of information – graphical/numerical.
Covered in 8.3.
Range: Type of application – those used for storing and presenting – graphical information – numerical information.
Covered in 8.3.
Range: Storage systems – existing and new systems established by the individual.
Covered by set tasks during assignment.
Range: Labelling conventions – existing and new conventions established by the individual.
Covered by set tasks during assignment.
Range: Type of systems option – facilities relating to the working environment.
Covered by set tasks during assignment.

Figure 6.6   Core skill checklist.

If you look closely at each of the performance criteria and the related range statements it is possible to highlight the core skills that could occur within this activity (see Figure 6.6). When looking at this checklist it is important to realize that a member of staff delivering any number of units within the programme has to consider several issues within their planning. These are:

- The unit(s)/element(s) to be delivered.
- The input required to assist students in their study.
- A core of resources.
- Ensure students have the opportunity to gain the grading themes.
- The core skills students have the opportunity to obtain through an activity.
- The forms of evidence to be submitted.
- The individual student action plan.

When students have met their action plan and submit work to be formally assessed, it has to be fully documented and cross-referenced with page or evidence references clearly indicated. To assist with the assessment a proforma was produced (see Figure 6.7).

Using this type of proforma, the assessor is able to record what the student has achieved and highlight any aspect that has been omitted. This enables the student to focus on what are hopefully small details, upgrade them and then resubmit by a new target date. It is essential that the proforma remains with the work at all times to assist in the internal and external verification processes.

Grading themes

The grading themes add another dimension to the delivery of GNVQ. During the pilot phase we left this out and it then became difficult to assess after the event. Students need to be encouraged to meet the needs of the grading criteria from the beginning. We have now included this within every activity/assignment proforma and ensure the relevant log for the level being studied is included. It assists in motivating the students because it gives an indication of how well a student is progressing. It must be noted that the grading criteria are the essence of good teaching practice and are never far away from a teacher's perceptions of what a student should be doing to achieve success. For the Advanced level the themes are:

School Logo	Name of School ACHIEVEMENTS AND ACTIONS	
Name/Date		Area/Level
UNITS		ELEMENTS

ELEMENT	P.C.	RANGE

ACTION

Next target date

STUDENT   ASSESSOR

Figure 6.7   Achievements & actions document.

- planning;
- information seeking and information handling;
- evaluation.

It is essential that the terms within these themes are understood by all who deliver the programmes, so ensuring standardization of work receiving a grade. To help us achieve this we were able to use a training day entitled 'Effective Learning' to discuss and formulate a common accord for the differences between a pass, a merit, and a distinction.

The process of working through the Advanced level Health and Social Care is similar for each of the units, whether they are delivered element by element, unit by unit or a combination of units. Planning the delivery framework is crucial to student success. Two years into the programme we have had numerous challenges to tackle and overcome, but we have also had some successes. To help in putting the 'pilot' phase into perspective it is worth mentioning some of the negative and positive aspects we have experienced.

Planning

Our initial planning was not very successful due to a number of constraints that were out of our control. It was not until March 1992 that we formally accepted the challenge to offer GNVQ in its 'pilot' phase. Our Awarding Body began a series of support workshops to assist us in the delivery of GNVQ. Unfortunately, like ourselves, they had very little extra information to impart in these initial stages and the perception that students could achieve the qualification through the Diploma of Vocational Education Preparatory Modules led everyone astray. From March to late June we spent all our planning time mapping out the similarities. It therefore came as a huge shock when at the end of June we were told this was no longer necessary. With only three weeks to go until the end of term and having already spent a number of training days on preparation which was effectively of no use to us, we felt frustrated, used and very concerned over the lack of effective planning that had been achieved.

Besides the constraints imposed through outside agencies, we also had to contend with internal constraints. The school timetable, staffing and meeting structure had already advanced to completion *before* it became evident that GNVQ was a completely different programme to implement. Due to this we had to work the GNVQ programmes on the Diploma of Vocational Education framework. This meant that out of a 50-hour fortnightly timetable only ten hours of teaching time had been allocated. Also the staffing structure did not allow for the rigour of standards set down for the assessment of these vocational courses. Lastly, the school meeting structure was already in place to cater for the Diploma not GNVQ, thus resulting in lack of contact time for individual vocational area team meetings. The support given by the Senior Management Team during the 'pilot' phase has been excellent without doubt, but even with this support it was realized that the first phase would be far from perfect. All of these issues would have a dramatic effect on the implementation of GNVQ.

Implementation

On starting to deliver the programme in September, 1992 it was realized that GNVQ was not quite as flexible as was at first thought. We found we had a mismatch of students on programmes, with some less able students taking two A levels alongside the vocational programme, so resulting in an overload of work. This progressively worsened as the students neared the end of their sixth-form studies and the knock-on effect was that students found it hard to complete all the necessary units for a full award. We were late starting the programmes, as not all documentation had been received, and this presented us with a further loss of time. Obviously there were a number of knock-on effects from the planning issues mentioned previously, plus the fact that we were continually receiving visits from a number of different agencies trying to collect data on the first phase of GNVQ. All of this took time to organize and that detracted from the time needed for essential planning. As we tried to come to terms with the specifications we found problems with the interpretation of different elements. The programme was far more knowledge-based and not so reliant on practical skills. If these were to be included staff had to try to find ways of introducing them. At the beginning we were not fully aware of the importance placed on evidence. This resulted in assessment problems as students did not always have visual evidence to support their claims. The other issue regarding assessment was the importance of cross-referencing every item of evidence so that an external verifier could find evidence quickly and easily when verifying portfolios. Lastly the testing. This caused no end of problems. Test papers did not always arrive on time, it took ages to receive the marks, and some questions were misleading to the students. The idea of students taking tests when ready did not materialize and we found ourselves having to have mini-examination sessions in order to fulfil the examination procedures given to us.

Consultation

The above paints a very gloomy picture, but remember it was a pilot phase. Everyone was in the same boat – HMIs, the awarding bodies, and schools and colleges alike. As we progressed so did our levels of knowledge and understanding; we were all going through a learning curve. One positive point was that in Dorset, five schools were involved in the pilot phase, and we were able to form a network which in the initial stages proved invaluable. We were able to discuss our problems, talk about subject-specific aspects and check on whether we had all received the same documentation through the post. No one provided any form of financial assistance during these stages but luckily our county provided some finance to be used to support the GNVQ developments. Things have improved over the past two years and we did have some successes as we went along.

Successes

Many of the problems associated with the pilot phase have been out of our control, but it is pleasing to note that we have had successes on which we wish to build. These definitely include the merging of Units 1 and 8 in Health and Social Care. Next time, students may plan something a little different from that noted here, but then that will enable the grading criteria to be claimed. The other successes have been the types of documentation that are being used. The Assignment/Activity proforma (Figure 6.3), the Matrix sheet (Figure 6.4) and the Achievements and Actions document (Figure 6.7) will all continue to be used, with some modifications. On the Assignment sheet (Figure 6.3) there are going to be two new headings on the Vocational Objectives sheets to cover the PCs and range, and on the Planning Sheet the headings will be changed to:

- Explanation of Action Plan and Revisions.
- The Information Sources Identified and Used.
- How the Evidence is Presented and Where it is to be Found.
- Student/Assessor Signature and Date.

On the Matrix sheet we are going to add a new column headed 'Activity Number' and change 'Assignment/Activity' to 'Performance Criteria'.

Many of the staff have been working towards their Training & Development Lead Body (TDLB) awards and this has assisted in understanding the processes within assessment and is helping to produce a variety of different forms of evidence. The staffing structure for delivering GNVQ has also been changed to accommodate the demands of the course. Each vocational area has a team leader who is responsible for monitoring student work and planning schemes of work. They have a number of staff under them who also assist in delivering the units of work. These vocational areas work with the internal verifier who is also the GNVQ co-ordinator.

If we were starting all over again, from scratch, I would definitely want to see the following in place, in order to ensure greater opportunity for student success:

- *Training of staff* to unpick the terminology and processes of GNVQ and start to set the standard.
- *Planning* to consider the order of unit delivery, the inclusion of the core skills and practical approaches *before* starting on GNVQ.
- *Staff structure* setting up team leaders for each vocational area, responsible for schemes of work and monitoring of student progress.
- *Meetings* for team leaders to meet with other assessors within the vocational area and for meetings with the GNVQ co-ordinator.
- *TDLB assessor awards*: staff to begin working towards these as soon as possible.
- *Resources* research and purchase of suitable texts to provide a basis for each unit of work as well as to provide equipment to assist in recording student evidence (e.g. video, dictaphones, camera, etc.).
- *Outside agencies* links to be made to support each of the units of work.
- *Guidance* offered in Year 11 must be explicit, highlighting the levels on offer, the entry requirements and the limitations of programmes, or combinations of programmes on offer.
- *Induction* must introduce students to the terminology and processes involved in GNVQ.
- *Monitoring* of student work is essential. Three stages need to be set up:
  1. student submits work for assessment, having referenced all evidence in a logical and understandable format;
  2. assessor checks all referenced work against the GNVQ Vocational and Core Specifications, and provides feedback for student;
  3. student/staff formulate new action plan to go on to new work or to revisit the work submitted which is not yet fully acceptable as evidence.

Much has been learnt from the pilot phase. Despite all the problems experienced, we are very positive about the future of GNVQ and look forward to building on our strengths and tackling the various challenges we still have to face. More importantly, it offers our students a programme of study suited to their needs, as was indicated by one of the students:

> GNVQ offered a style of learning more suited to my needs, enabling me to work at my own pace. Much of the study relies on individual investigations which have developed my skills of research, planning and evaluation.

A very positive quotation on which to end!

Chapter 7

RICHARD HEWLETT # GNVQ in Leisure and Tourism

Introduction

GLOSCAT is a large further education college situated in Chelten-ham and Gloucester with approximately 3,500 full-time students and 31,500 part-time students. It is organized into faculties and schools with Leisure and Tourism in the School of Languages. GLOSCAT was involved from the start in the piloting of the GNVQ in Leisure and Tourism and currently has approximately 60 students on the Intermediate and 140 on the Advanced programme. The first GNVQ Advanced students graduated in June 1994, with the majority progressing into jobs or Higher Education.

The introduction of the GNVQ in Leisure and Tourism brought together two major areas of the curriculum which had not generally worked closely together before. There was initially a large degree of scepticism that the two areas could be brought together successfully and that students on the programme would have a worthwhile learning experience that would prepare them for further study or employment. Much of our initial debate about joining the Pilot programme centred around these issues and it is fair to say that many of the arguments still rumble on today within programme teams. Once the decision to join the pilot phase was made there were immediately a number of key decisions that needed to be taken before detailed planning and implementation could take place.

Key Planning Decisions

Delivery methods

The GNVQ guidelines issued by the validating bodies wanted a major change in delivery methods for a number of course teams, particularly those that had been involved with BTEC programmes up until the introduction of GNVQs. The BTEC philosophy had been to integrate subject areas as much as possible to make the qualification coherent and relevant to employment. To this end integrated assignments were encouraged to achieve learning objectives across a number of subject areas and to develop skills. GNVQs were radically different from this in that they were written in a modular format with each free-standing unit containing elements and performance criteria that, in theory, could be taught and achieved in isolation by a student without reference to any other units. With no real delivery guidelines from the validation bodies it was left to individual programme teams to decide on the best delivery method. It was realized early on that there would need to be some clear college-wide delivery decisions made for all GNVQ programmes so that they would all run within the same yearly timetable structure and could link with other qualifications. This was achieved through a GNVQ Steering Group. Programme delivery, however, varied from area to area. In Leisure and Tourism it was decided to go for a fully modular programme where Business Studies developed an integrated delivery system. No system is perfect and we have found the following advantages and disadvantages with our modular scheme (see Figures 7.1a and b).

Advantages

- It allows maximum student flexibility with programmes and allows the development of individual learning programmes tailored specifically to student needs. (This is always subject to some timetable restraints.)
- The guidelines seem to be written for modular delivery, which makes this method easily understood by students and staff alike.
- It allows for effective use of teaching resources and potential efficiency gains in the management of programmes.
- There is a reduction in the need for specialist staff participating for some mandatory subjects (i.e. Customer Care can be made relevant to all students using examples from what used to be two separate subject areas).
- There is an improvement in communication with programme teams and with the recording and tracking of individual students.

		Block 1	Block 2	Block 3	GP TUT
GNVQ Level II	Group 2/1/1 Leisure	2LT1 2LT9 2HSC4	2LT3 2LT12 2LT7	2LT4 2LT2 2LT8	PG
	Group 2/1/2 Tourism	2LT1 2LT8 2LT2	2LT4 2HSC4 2LT6*	2LT3 2LT9 2LT7	PT
	Group 2/1/3 Leisure	2LT1 2LT9 2LT4	2LT2 2LT8 2LT12	2LT3 2LT7 2HSC4	EM

		Block 1	Block 2	Block 3	
GNVQ Level III Year I	Group 3/1(1)1 Leisure	3LT1 3LT3 LT015	C 3LT5 LT09	3LT2 PI 3LT4	PC
	Group 3/1(1)2 Tourism	3LT1 3LT4 LT015	PI LT016 3LT3	LT09 3LT5 LT017	PB
	Group 3/1(1)3 Tourism	3LT1 3LT4 LT015	3LT3 3LT5 LT09	LT013 3LT2	MW
	Group 3/1(1)4 Tourism	3LT1 3LT3 LT011	LT013 LT016 T.S.	3LT5 LT09 LT017	RL

		Block 1	Block 2	Block 3	
GNVQ Level III Year II 94/5	Group 3/5(2)1 Leisure	3LT2 LT017 3LT7	3LT6 3LT8 PII	LT010 E	PC
	Group 3/5(2)2 Tourism	3LT6 LT017 LT010	3LT2 3LT7 3LT8	PII E	JL
	Group 3/5(2)3 Tourism	3LT2 LT017 3LT7	3LT6 3LT8 K	*B A	MW
	Group 3/5(2)4 Tourism	3LT6 LT017 A	3LT2 3LT8 3LT7	*G K	ST

Figure 7.1(a)   Modular timetable.

Disadvantages

- There is an increased need for detailed central planning at an early stage (i.e. when modules are to be taught), and when decisions are agreed there is little scope for changing them later in the programme. It is a paradox that, in order to allow students maximum flexibility, it is necessary to have very rigid delivery programmes which are in place early.
- Communication needs to be accurate and well co-ordinated particularly if there are links across programme areas in order

Intermediate – Mandatory

2LT1 Investigating Leisure and Tourism
2LT2 Contributing to an Event or Service
2LT3 Customer Service
2LT4 Promoting Products and Service

Options

2LT5 Developing Leisure Products & Services
2LT6 Researching Tourism Destinations
2LT7 Operational Practices in the Leisure and Tourism Industries
2LT8 Investigate the Environmental Impact of Leisure and Tourism

Additional Units

2LT12 CSLA
2HSC4 First Aid/Lifesaving
2LT9   Health & Fitness

Advanced – Mandatory Units

3LT1 Investigating the Leisure and Tourism Industry
3LT2 Maintaining Health, Safety and Security
3LT3 Providing Customer Service
3LT4 Marketing in Leisure and Tourism
3LT5 Planning for an Event or Function
3LT6 Providing Management Information Service
3LT7 Working in Teams
3LT8 Evaluating the Performance of Facilities

Optional Units

LT09   Human Resource issues in the Leisure and Tourism Industry
LT010 Applying Marketing & Media Techniques in Leisure and Tourism
LT011 Investigating Travel Organizers
LT013 Investigating the UK Holiday Industry
LT015 Investigating Leisure Facility Operations
LT016 Foreign Language (Listening L2)
LT017 Foreign Language (Oral S2)

Additional Units

A	Travel, Tourism & Geography –	2850K	K	Third World Tourism
B	Leisure Travel Services –	2851K	P1	Principles of Sports Coaching I
C	Sports and Physical Recreation –	2852K	P2	Principles of Sports Coaching II
G	Business Travel –	2855K	E	Health-Related Fitness
T.S.	Travel Services –			

Figure 7.1(b) Modular timetable reference sheet.

to co-ordinate option choices.
- Subjects such as A levels do not fit well into a GNVQ modular programme because of their radically different methods of delivery and assessment.
- It can be expensive to set up the planning and monitoring mechanism needed for a GNVQ programme.

- There can be a number of areas of overlap within modules which can duplicate teaching and affect student motivation.

Package offered (student entitlement)

It is important that an early decision is made on student entitlement for all levels of the GNVQ programme – for instance, in the advanced GNVQ the minimum requirement is for 12 units (eight mandatory and four optional) and this is seen as roughly equivalent to two A levels. Any provision above this is at the discretion of the programme organizer and in a number of cases they provide up to 18 units which is the equivalent of three A levels. It is felt that this extra provision will give students wishing to enter higher education the best choice and allow students wishing to go into employment the opportunity to pick up specialist units such as First Aid or Life-saving which will help them find a job. The aim, then, of the extra units, is to allow maximum student choice so a combination of GNVQ, NVQ, A level and vocational units should be offered within the given resource constraints (module timetable and modular reference sheets provided).

Changes to the FEFC funding model may make the 18-unit model difficult to provide for all students in the future and, in some cases, the 12-unit model may be appropriate. It is still not entirely clear what GNVQ combination is the most appropriate for students wishing to enter higher education with each institution making its own decisions. As GNVQs become better known and more accepted this situation should improve, but it has been a difficult problem for the students involved in the pilot.

Recruitment

Recruitment policy for the GNVQ in Leisure and Tourism has evolved with each new intake. Initially, recruitment was based upon students identifying the level of GNVQ they wished to be considered for (e.g. Advanced in Leisure and Tourism), and which 'stream' they wished to follow (i.e. Leisure or Tourism). The process of marketing, interviewing and induction was based around this model and students were allocated to groups very early on in the course. Experience has led to a number of changes taking place and now the key areas of recruitment policies are:

- The whole GNVQ Leisure and Tourism programme is marketed with the message that we have the right level of course for *any* student wishing to study in the area of Leisure or Tourism

(Foundation, Intermediate and Advanced levels are on offer). This effectively guarantees students who interview effectively a place on the course even if they don't achieve the expected results in any GCSE exams.

- All students are put through an extended induction programme which aims to place them on the right level for their needs and ability and to define their own individual learning programme from within the programme offered. Students can and do move between levels, often at their own request, so tutor groups are not usually confirmed until the end of induction.

Working with the Specifications

The specification for GNVQ in Leisure and Tourism attempted to bring together two different sectors with very different requirements and to form a coherent programme that would be relevant to students in both areas. In the pilot phase the eight mandatory units formed the core of the qualification with a small range of optional units available to make up the 12 units. At this point a number of units were still in the process of accreditation by NCVQ so choice was very limited. One interesting point to note is that languages (two units) were available for the Leisure and Tourism programme as optional units, whereas with most other qualifications they were offered as additional units.

The specifications themselves were in a standard format which was familiar to anybody experienced in NVQ programmes. Unfortunately, very few Leisure and Tourism tutors had experience with the qualification so the language of 'elements', 'performance criteria' and 'range statements' was a new and frightening one. It very quickly became apparent that very little of the material developed for BTEC National Diploma programmes could be used for GNVQ. The main reason for this was the need to show specific evidence for the achievement of the performance criteria and to demonstrate that the whole of the range had been covered. This process was alien to many tutors and it has taken two years to develop materials that are achieving the desired results.

Another radical departure was the assessment process that was to be used for GNVQs. It was made up of three parts of differing importance:

(a) There was the requirement that a student must demonstrate achievement of all of the elements and the performance criteria within the elements across the range stated in the unit. This evidence, when assessed, went towards the portfolio which was used for the third stage of assessment.

(b) Each mandatory unit (this was reduced to seven in Year 2 of the course) had an externally set test at the end which demonstrated coverage of the whole unit and a basic level of knowledge achieved. It had a high pass mark (initially 80 per cent reduced to 70 per cent) and was described as a 'gate' through which the student must pass to get to the third stage of assessment. The end test had to be passed before the student was credited with the unit so, in a number of cases, the 'gate' became a brick wall which stopped student progress. Many of the initial end tests were of poor quality and did not stick to the knowledge areas that had been indicated. They have, however, undergone rapid development and now provide a fair test of student knowledge and achievement.

(c) If a student achieves both (a) and (b) they are then in a position to have their qualification graded at Pass, Merit or Distinction against a set of process-skills criteria based on Planning, Information Seeking and Gathering and (at Advanced level) Evaluation. This is probably the most controversial area of assessment and the one that tutors and students find the most difficulty with. In practice a number of different approaches have been taken to this area of assessment. Ideally, this should be done when all the evidence is available in the portfolio. In practice, however, this has often proved to be impossible with students amassing large quantities of work over a two-year course, and the need for interim guides as the course progresses. Most programme teams now produce some form of regular indicative grading of the portfolio work with a confirmation of the grades at the end of the course.

The process as it stands at the moment only produces one overall grade for the whole qualification with no further grading at all for any additional units that are achieved. This is seen by many as highly unsatisfactory and the preference would be for a system where each unit receives a grade, thus giving each student a graded profile for the qualification.

Working with the specifications has been further complicated by the current changes that are being made to all aspects of the programme. The unit specifications have been changed every year and the grading criteria are in the process of change in order to reflect more the content of the work being assessed. Many of the changes are necessary and welcome, but it does increase the stress on programme teams who constantly need to change assignments and the way in which they assess student work.

Core skills

Core skills are an important element of the qualification and each student is required to complete successfully a minimum of three (Communication, Information Technology, Application of Number), and to achieve them at least at the same level as the qualifications BTEC describe them as:

> Personal Transferable Skills which play an important part in developing the effective performance of the individual in a wide range of vocational contexts . . . core skills are those generic skills which are used in carrying out all tasks and activities, whether in education and training, at work or in life in general.

The core-skills units are written in the same format as other GNVQ units with elements, performance criteria and range statements, and across all of the five levels.

It was the initial aim of the programme team in the pilot to develop and assess the core skills as an integrated part of the overall delivery of the course. It was felt that enough opportunities could be found for students to achieve their core skills through the programme of assignments that were being developed, and for them to use evidence from external sources if it was relevant. As the course progressed it became apparent that not all of the skills could be achieved in this way. This was particularly true for Application of Number and Information Technology, but for different reasons. It soon became clear that the Information Technology skills required were not being developed systematically in the core modules and that there was no unit specifically related to IT. Students with little or no IT skills prior to the courses were not able to achieve their core-skills unit and hence would fail the whole qualification. To overcome this, independent lessons on IT skills were developed which also undertook some of the assessment requiring direct observation of skills. This has now become a standard feature of all our Leisure and Tourism GNVQ courses.

The problem with Application of Number centred around applying some of the numerical concepts that needed to be assessed to realistic Leisure and Tourism contexts in the assignments. The most notorious example was probably Pythagoras's theorem (since withdrawn) but there were a number of other examples that could only be achieved through very controversial assignment briefs. To overcome this, a workshop approach was adopted for those number skills not easily achieved. Members of staff specializing in number devised exercises to assess them. Initially these exercises were not always in context and were used across a number of GNVQ programmes, but development of these has put them all into the Leisure and Tourism context for current students.

The whole process for claiming core skills has developed over the lifetime of the qualification. It has become more and more the students' responsibility to provide the evidence of achievement which is then verified by staff. Everybody found this concept difficult at first, mainly because of the complex language in which the core skills were written and, in many cases, they had to be rewritten into language that was clear to both students and tutors. Also, because it was difficult, a number of students left the claiming of core skills to the end of the course and then had a great deal of difficulty finding the evidence and tutors to verify it. Our current scheme calls for the systematic collection of skills over the whole length of the course with regular checks by tutors of programmes; there still, however, seems to be panic at the end of the year!

Students who achieve their core skills at the required level before the completion of the course should be given the opportunity to progress and achieve at a higher level. This has been very difficult to implement in the pilot stage where the main difficulty was getting achievement at the required level. In order to address this in future, we are extending the concept of the workshop to include those who wish to develop the higher-level skills. They will be able to access specially devised exercises and will be able to ask for assessment against the higher-level performance criteria.

Core skills has been one of the most difficult areas to develop and has probably caused the most problems to students in understanding it and being able to gather evidence. The lessons we have drawn from this are:

1. Ensure that students realize the importance of core skills to their overall qualification.
2. Ensure that the core-skills language is understood. Translate the performance criteria and give examples of evidence if necessary.
3. Develop a mechanism for claiming and recording core skills which is understood both by students and tutors.

4. Identify clearly which skills can be achieved through the main programme and which used to be achieved through other means (workshops etc.).

5. Develop in the students a systematic approach to core-skills claiming through regular tutorials and progress checks.

6. Allow students the opportunity to claim core skills using evidence from outside the course programme (e.g. evidence from part-time work etc.). This evidence has to be verifiable and clearly identified with specific performance indicators.

7. Develop a specialist team of staff for core skills. They need to be familiar with the claiming mechanisms and how to accredit for prior learning with students.

8. Many students see the core skills as a continuation of the old Maths and English lessons and so have a fairly negative attitude towards them. This can be overcome to some extent by developing them through realistic vocational examples that have relevance to the students' course of study.

External tests

A new feature of the GNVQ was the introduction of the external test for all mandatory units which had to be passed before the unit could be awarded. The external test concept was common to all GNVQ irrespective of the validating body, but initially the form that this test took varied from body to body. The aim of this test was to ensure that the underpinning skills and knowledge for a unit had been achieved across the whole of the range and was thought of as the minimum amount of knowledge a student would need to have to meet the requirements of the unit. For this reason, the pass mark was initially set at 80 per cent, although this was subsequently reduced to 70 per cent as it became apparent that the higher mark was unrealistic for most students.

The external tests were controversial from the start for two main reasons. Firstly, the validation bodies and NCVQ stated from the start that centres should not teach towards the external test requirements and that they were only a 'gateway' through which the student must pass in order for their work to be assessed for an overall grade. This had to be considered against the fact that students' work couldn't be given an overall grade until all of the mandatory unit end tests (later one unit end test was dropped) had been passed. It quickly became apparent that the end tests were of great importance and must be passed, and most course teams did teach to, and set up revision sessions for, the external tests and this has, to a large extent, continued throughout the course.

The second major problem was the format of the tests and the way in which they were written. The rapid introduction of the qualification had left little time for test development, and this showed in the early test papers which had badly written and, sometimes, wrong questions which often did not conform to the knowledge specifications that had been accredited. It is fair to say, however, that lessons were learnt quickly in this area and there was a rapid improvement in the standard of papers. Now the majority are multiple-choice, machine-marketable tests which allow fast turnaround times.

A number of lecturers were extremely apprehensive about the end tests because of the effects they may have on student motivation on the course. A number of students had 'failed' under the traditional examination scheme at GCSE and were looking for a course where they could be continuously assessed on assignment work as they were on traditional National Diploma courses. The GNVQ reintroduced the exam element and in the initial stages large numbers of students were failing these tests. We were surprised to find that most students were not de-motivated by failure; they realized that they could take the exams again and that they were not the only ones having problems – some even said they like the tests as an indication of how well they were doing on the course.

From a course-management perspective, the external tests are extremely disruptive to the programme as a whole. On a modular scheme the timing is not correct for the teaching pattern and generally a week is lost for each testing period. The week prior to the tests is usually taken up with some form of revision so, again, normal lessons are disrupted. Students can re-sit the tests as many times as they need (under current regulations) which can lead to a build-up of examinations in the re-sit weeks. All of the tests and results need to be carefully tracked and checked to ensure that all students have the required number at the end of the course (there is an added complication when unit specification and hence external tests change halfway through the course).

The external tests have improved and student performance on them has got better. It has been proposed that they will be available on demand from the validation body and this will improve the course management element and allow proper programming. They do give the qualification external credibility and challenge the student with the need for a basic knowledge requirement across the whole range of the course.

Links with other qualifications

It is a feature of the GNVQ that it can be linked with other qualifications in order to provide students with an individualized tailor-made vocational package best suited to their career needs. This is obviously limited by the size of provision available and timetabling constraints that may appear. If a student is studying the basic 12-unit GNVQ then any additionality units can take one of four forms:

1. *Extra GNVQ units.* These can be taken from the optional or additional units offered with the Leisure and Tourism or from any other GNVQ programme. In practice this does not work out on a 'free-for-all pick and mix' programme, and students are carefully tutored to pick those units that are relevant to their future career needs. A point to note is that, under current regulations, if a student studies a mandatory unit from another area which requires an end test, they must pass that end test before they can claim the unit even though it doesn't count towards the mandatory unit requirement for Leisure and Tourism.
2. *A levels.* In most cases it is possible to combine one A level with a GNVQ programme. Again, the A level selected needs to complement the overall GNVQ. There are major differences in timetabling, study methods and assessment between the two areas and students need to be aware of this. The introduction of modular A levels may help to rectify this but these are not yet universally available in all subjects.
3. *NVQ units.* For students with a clear vocational aim it is possible for them to start on NVQ qualifications as an addition to their GNVQ. These are much more vocationally oriented and most require a large amount of work-based assessment. They can, however, be started in college and some elements achieved. These are particularly useful for students wishing to enter employment after the qualification (e.g. NVQ Travel Services).
4. *Other qualifications.* There are a range of additional qualifications which are not yet covered by the NCVQ framework that are none the less extremely useful to the employment prospects of students. These would include first-aid awards, lifesaving awards and specialist tourism qualifications such as ABTA and Green Badge Grading courses.

Most programmes make some allowance for additional units and the one selected will depend very much on the student's future plans. In general the GNVQ and A-level option is most useful for those wishing to enter higher education and the other option for those wishing to go straight into employment.

Verification

The verification processes introduced for GNVQ were again relatively new to a number of staff, and their importance was probably not realized by a number of people at the beginning of the qualification. The process is split into two main areas, with internal verifiers appointed by the centre to control the internal assessment processes and external verifiers appointed by the validating body to check that the centre is assessing properly and to update teams on current best practice. In operation the system is comprehensive and ensures that every aspect of work is examined. It was not appreciated at first how long this would take, nor the amount of time allocated to internal verification, and we currently have a team of five lecturers each with one hour per week on their timetable for the full academic year to internally verify approximately 180 full-time Intermediate and Advanced students.

Another major consideration is the training requirement for verification. The necessary qualifications are difficult to obtain, expensive and will probably soon become compulsory.

Student experience on the courses

The rapid introduction of the pilot GNVQ in Leisure and Tourism meant that many students had little idea of what this new qualification was and how it would enable them to progress. When the decision to run the course was made we undertook careful counselling sessions with students to explain about the new qualification (what little we knew at that stage), and to reassure them of its value. These main concerns could be summarized under three headings:

1. *Are we guinea pigs*? Many students rightly perceived that they were going to be guinea pigs on the course and that there was, initially, much confusion from all parties as to what was required from them. This situation persisted for much of the first year and into the second with the radical revisions which were made on the programme by NCVQ. Student feedback indicates that much of the confusion had been overcome by the middle of Year 2 and that they were happy with the final outcome of the course. One advantage of the pilot was that students were

always given the benefit of the doubt on the course so that problems did not affect the outcome of their qualification.

2. *Validity of qualification.* As with all new qualifications, there is a worry over the currency it will have in the education market-place. This was especially true for the Advanced qualification which would be used by students wishing to enter higher education. A great deal of effort went into advising HE establishments on the merits of the new qualification in order to give students a fair hearing when they applied. The outcome of this has been generally favourable, with most GNVQ students receiving offers for HE and a high level of awareness about GNVQ from most HE admissions tutors.

3. *Assessment.* Assessment problems centred around the end-test requirements, the putting together of a portfolio and the use of grading themes to arrive at an overall qualification grade. The end-test situation improved throughout the course as the tests themselves improved and students became more accustomed to doing them. The makings of a portfolio became clear as new guidelines were produced, but there were ongoing problems with the grading themes and their relevance to the qualification outcome. Many students wished to see some recognition of content in the grading themes which is likely to be addressed in future versions of the qualification.

Our final feedback session with the students indicated a high degree of satisfaction with the course, and they had noticed major improvements in the management and organization of the course and were satisfied that they had a worthwhile qualification despite well-publicized views to the contrary. The take-up of the students into higher education and employment is encouraging with an ever-widening appreciation of what a GNVQ qualification involves for the student. The qualification has changed and developed a great deal over the two years of its existence. Students and staff have adapted quickly to different methods of delivery and assessment with much rewriting of course materials and vetting of delivery methods. It is the opinion of most staff that the qualification is now broader in content but more rigorous in assessment than any that went before, and that if taught with integrity it will prepare students well for their future careers. Quality control by the validation bodies will be crucial in ensuring that standards are developed, maintained and improved across all the bodies, and that a few poorly run schemes do not affect the credibility of the whole qualification. There is a real opportunity to have a credible alternative to A levels for the more practically and vocationally oriented students, and this must not be lost or allowed to be damaged by bad publicity.

Activities

To provide a flavour of the type of activities Leisure and Tourism students are involved in, two sample assignments are included.

The assignment titled 'Customer Care Programme' was one that we used in the early stages of the GNVQ programme. This is very much in line with the BTEC National assignments. We were advised by our FEFC inspectors that these old-style assignment briefs were too vague for GNVQ. The result has been the development of all assignments in the format given for 'Alton Towers'. The assignment brief is used alongside the BTEC 'Assessment Specification' which gives details of elements, performance criteria, range and evidence indicators for the vocational content, and element and range for the core skills. Linked to the assignment brief for 'Alton Towers' is a detailed evidence/task sheet. This provides the additional guidance as advised by the inspectors. This detail almost guarantees that students will achieve a pass if they follow the steps as detailed. We are conscious of the danger of over-prescription and thereby reducing the potential for individual activity for the achievement of merit or distinction. The team is closely monitoring the situation to ensure that students will be stretched and will be able to evidence their grading themes.

GNVQ Advanced level Leisure and Tourism

A customer care programme

Scenario

In Assignment 1 you looked at an establishment's customers and their perception of the customer care they received. The second assignment will build upon this experience by asking you to produce a new customer care programme for the area you investigated which will include your recommendations from the evaluation of the existing programme.

Students will need to stay in the same working groups as Assignment 1 but MUST perform different tasks from Assignment 1. The group must then carry out the following tasks.

Task 1

The group will need to look at the evaluation of Assignment 1 and identify an area of customer care that is not achieving the desired results (e.g. telephone technique, face-to-face communication, customer information). When this has been identified and agreed with the tutor, the group will need to:

(a) Plan a customer care programme that is practical and justified and which will improve this problem area.
(b) Identify how the programme would be implemented to include
  • the range of people involved;
  • the training needs of those people and how the training would take place;
  • the cost implication of the programme;
  • how its effectiveness will be monitored.

Task 2

The plan will need to be submitted in report form to the head of the unit along with a ten-minute demonstration of one of the training needs for the new programme.
  EACH STUDENT WILL, IN ADDITION, NEED TO SUBMIT THEIR INDIVIDUAL ASSIGNMENT PLANNER FOR THE ASSIGNMENT.

Assessment criteria

To achieve a **Pass** for the assignment the group must have achieved all items in Tasks 1 and 2. These results, plus the Assignment Planner, will be used to determine the portfolio grades.

GNVQ Advanced Leisure and Tourism

Maintaining health, safety and security: 'Alton Towers'

Evidence

An individually produced informal report which has been word processed.

Background information

As part of your second-year induction programme you will be going on a visit to Alton Towers. For your first health, safety and security assignment you will have to investigate several aspects of Alton

Towers' operations but this must be done *without* asking questions of the staff at the theme park or writing to staff for additional information. The assignment is intended to give you a thorough overview of the existing health, safety and security arrangements at a theme park and also to encourage you to suggest ways in which they could be improved or extended. The second health, safety and security assignment will focus on the legal and regulatory requirements which affect leisure and tourism facilities.

Elements and performance criteria covered

Element 2.2: Propose ways of enhancing the health and safety of customers and staff
Performance criteria:

2.2.1   current and potential health and safety hazard situations and their causes are identified;

2.2.2   sources of expert help and advice are identified, described and used when necessary;

2.2.3   hazards are assessed for the probability and severity of harm, using relevant sources of information/advice;

2.2.4   proposals are made for any realistic measures necessary to enhance health and safety;

2.2.5   proposals are consistent with relevant legal and regulatory requirements and customer expectations;

2.2.6   proposed measures are accurately costed and resource implications are viable.

Element 2.3: Propose ways of enhancing security in leisure and tourism
Performance criteria

2.3.1   current and potential security hazards and their causes are identified;

2.3.2   sources of expert help and advice are identified, described and used when necessary;

2.3.3   security hazards are assessed for probability and level of loss using relevant sources of information/advice;

2.3.4   proposals are made for any realistic measures necessary to enhance security;

2.3.5   proposals are consistent with relevant legal requirements and customer expectations;

2.3.6   proposed measures are accurately costed and resource implications are viable;

2.3.7   measures proposed are logistically viable for the event, product or service;

2.3.8   all information and proposals are handled with due regard to confidentiality.

Tasks

P.C.: 2.2.1, 2.2.3

(a) An explanation of the main causes and likely scale of the threats to health and safety at a theme park (e.g. litter and badly maintained rides are both threats to health and safety but how likely are each to occur and how big a problem would they cause?).

P.C.: 2.3.1, 2.3.3

(b) An explanation of the main causes and likely scale of the threats to security at a theme park.

P.C.: 2.2.1, 2.3.1

(c) A description of any examples of health, safety and security problems you observed when you were at Alton Towers.

P.C.: 2.2.1, 2.3.1

(d) A description of any health, safety and security problems which have occurred at Alton Towers or other theme parks which have been reported in the media. (NB. You will need to state where and when the incidents occurred.)

P.C.: 2.2.2, 2.3.2

(e) A description of how the management team of Alton Towers could obtain expert help and advice in maintaining the health, safety and security of the theme park. List these sources of help and advice, giving contact details where possible.

P.C.: 2.2.4, 2.3.4

(f) A description and explanation of the measures taken at a theme park to reduce the risks of each of the hazards to health, safety and security that you mentioned in tasks (a)(b)(c) and (d).

(g) A description and explanation of any *further* measures you would suggest to improve the health, safety and security arrangements at a theme park together with:
   - your reasons for suggesting them;
   - realistic costings and resource implications (e.g. skills of staff, availability, extra staff, etc.);
   - an explanation of how these measures meet the legal and regulatory requirements for health, safety and security as well as what is expected by customers.

(*NB.* To do this properly you will need to find out what the legal requirements for health, safety and security in leisure and tourism facilities are and refer to them in your answer.)

In addition to these sections, your report should also include sections to help you achieve the portfolio grades.

(i) *Planning.* This section should explain what you did in preparation for the visit in order to gather the information needed and also an action plan explaining everything you would need to do to complete the whole assignment successfully.

(ii) *Information gathering.* This section should include a checklist of what you looked for during your visit and any other sources of information you used in your assignment, plus comments on how reliable and valid you felt the information to be.

(iii) *Evaluation.* This section should explain why you approached the assignment as you did and how effective you felt this approach to be.

This is an **individual** assignment although you may choose to research different aspects and then swap information with other students.

Suggestions

Included below is a list of some of the aspects of health, safety and security you should include in this assignment. (*NB.* This list should be used only as a guide and *should* be expanded upon.)

(a) *Health and Safety*
- food hygiene;
- litter;
- first aid;
- toilets;
- clothing and safety equipment for staff;
- legal requirements covering theme parks and other leisure and tourism facilities;
- emergency procedures and equipment;
- hazardous situations observed whilst visiting;
- hazardous substances used on site and their storage;
- use of signs for health and safety purposes.

(b) *Security*
- ticket forgery;
- physical barriers;
- shop-lifting from catering outlets, gift shops, etc.;
- car park security.

This assignment should be submitted at _____ on _____
to _____ in _____
Any assignment handed in after this date and time may result in you failing this course.
This assignment **must be** retained for your portfolio.

Chapter 8

GEORGE PATTISON # GNVQ in Manufacturing

Introduction

The school piloted the Intermediate level GNVQ Manufacturing course in 1992/93 and based on that experience planned the next year's course in the summer term of 1993. This chapter therefore relates to two years of practice. Inherent in this practice is a greater understanding of the objectives and potential of the GNVQ course, how assessment and student tracking can be improved and how to minimize paperwork without jeopardizing the opportunity for good supporting evidence.

Basics

The nature of GNVQ requires evidence to ensure that processes, tasks and assignments have been carried out. GNVQ is not a NVQ where there is emphasis on skill acquisition. It is our experience that most of our students will choose a GNVQ in Manufacturing as their present interest is in practical matters. The skill in setting up a successful course must therefore be in achieving a balance between the practical and the written. Linked to this are standards. A pass at Intermediate level of GNVQ is equivalent for four GCSEs. To obtain four GCSEs it is inferred that students must have a reasonable level of core skills, or be motivated to develop these. Inherent in GNVQ is the opportunity to obtain merits or distinctions.

If these requirements are considered when planning a course, it is evident that there must be a considerable amount of structure and assistance for the student throughout, whilst providing the opportunity for individual initiative.

Experience suggests that paperwork should be available from an IT source whenever possible, thus freeing up time for practical assignments.

Where to start

Teachers involved in practical subjects find the construction and assessment of practical assignments comparatively easy. For ease of administration, where possible, assignments or tasks should relate to discrete units or elements of units. However, in Manufacturing this is made more difficult as a practical assignment may span a number of units.

Planning for practice

Based on running a pilot GNVQ in Manufacturing in the previous year, and having gained a degree of confidence and experience, certain decisions were made.

1. To organize the course on the strengths of the school and the Design and Technology department.
2. To identify the key elements such as work experience, review dates, holidays, end tests and assessment of coursework and incorporate these into a year plan.
3. To consider how the units will be taught and the implications for teaching staff.
4. To decide how the core will be taught.
5. To decide on the allocation of student time: contact with teachers and self-supported study.
6. To examine the detail of the units
   (a) to create a more detailed framework based on work 'sketched in';
   (b) to ensure that the whole course will be covered;
   (c) to link the units with the teaching of the core.
7. To ensure that the assignments supported the unit end test.

1. Practical assignments

Based on the pilot, we decided that where possible we would aim for a degree of reality rather than use simulations in practical assignments. The outcomes were to have real implications. Initially we considered adopting Young Enterprise but we opted for an in-house mini-enterprise scheme involving staff and students.

As we had good metal-casting facilities we decided on an assignment using casting. Other assignments were based on standard

Design and Technology facilities. We expected no more than 15 students to enrol for the course.

2. Key elements in year planning

The year was split (see Figure 8.1). The intention was to have some form of general GNVQ induction across all the vocational areas. However, on starting this was left to the Manufacturing team. In retrospect, induction is an area for development.

In addition to the continuous assessment of assignments it was decided to have two comprehensive reviews and to use the third term to prepare for the final assessment and display of work. The objective therefore was to cover the bulk of the course in two terms (30 weeks). The display of practical work and graphics with supporting

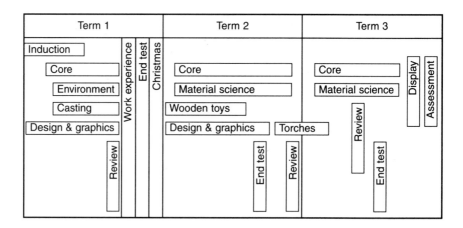

Figure 8.1 Planning for a year's work.

documentation provided the basis for the reviews. It was considered impossible to teach Manufacturing in neatly boxed units and elements and thus reviews would be based on assignments rather than units. It was doubly important that students should see their progress in terms of the whole course, and log sheets were written up at the end of each assignment.

Work experience was organized for three weeks before the Christmas break. The previous year's work experience had been timed for January but we found this interrupted the flow of the course. A longer second term was preferred.

End test dates were set by the awarding body and we decided that all candidates should enter Units 2 to 4 in December as their practical assignments covered all the issues within these units. The role of the co-ordinator was recognized as crucial, particularly so at

the beginning of the third term where there were a number of
teaching staff involved in cross-linking themes and there was a need
to ensure that all units and elements were covered. Student work
needed to be reviewed in detail to ensure that late or missed
assignments were dealt with. The importance of student and course
reviews on a formal regular basis is self-evident.

3. Units and staff

Building a course involving many staff is an interactive process.
Our model was firstly to select the optional units and use these and
the mandatory units to compile the main assignments. The initial
work was outlined, and, based on agreed or projected contact time
with students and possible unit groupings, a matrix was compiled
based on 30 weeks. These were roughly grouped into units of Design,
Unit 1; Graphics, Unit 5; Manufacturing Systems, part Unit 2;
Making, Units 2 to 4; and the Environment and Materials, part Unit
4 and Unit 6. Additionally, one hour was allocated to part of Unit 2
for the review and planning of assignments.

The outline organized, the detailed writing of the course could
commence. Ideally, each team member should write their own part
and establish cross-links. In the event, the cross-linking was carried
out informally. For example, towards the end of the casting project
students had to deal with a simulated letter of complaint from a
business customer. Although this emanated from the practical
work, the discussion and writing of the letters were carried out in
Communication core time. The students had enough experience in
the practical work to understand the complaint and produce an
appropriate response. It may be worth noting that if this had been
arranged on a formal basis the timing may not have been optimal.
Good team building within the delivery team is useful in facilitating
the development of a new course.

4. Teaching the core

It was thought that specialist teachers should teach core skills to
give due emphasis to their importance within the course. Both
integration and separate teaching have advantages. If the delivery
team is well integrated, and able to provide continuity within an
established programme, there are advantages in complementary in-
depth study for progression and support. Equally, if a course is well-
established one can organize core study into the assignments, with
perhaps advice from a specialist. The third option is one where both

the core specialist and the deliverer of practical studies complement the work of each other. For example, the teaching of spreadsheets or databases may initially be carried out by a specialist. If the student has access to suitable computers within the practical area there may then be the possibility of using databases in a variety of ways. For example, for control of stocks, progressing an order, planning resources of personnel, equipment or materials and asking the 'what if' questions.

5. Timetabling

A decision was made to give a high level of teacher support and contact time to our GNVQ courses. A basic requirement was the allocation of two- to three-hour blocks for practical assignments, preferably in the morning, thus ensuring that team production runs could be successfully undertaken. This was essential and was an improvement over the pilot year. However, when this was not possible, and a teacher saw a student for only one hour per week, the coursework suffered. This will be referred to later in more detail. There is a Learning Support Centre within the school and students were expected to use this in their free time. The number of hours allocated to each unit is outlined in the section on the teaching team.

6. Detailed planning of assignments: case study – an electric torch

This in some ways was a classic Craft, Design and Technology (CDT) design-and-make assignment with the additional opportunity for working both co-operatively and independently. As it was time-tabled for the second term, certain factors favoured it as a cross-unit assignment:

- The practical work could follow the initial design work, although two teachers were teaching it.
- Students already had experience of production issues and were familiar with the terminology. It also had the advantage of including an assembly operation.
- Students had the opportunity to bring many more of their own ideas as to how the assignment should be organized.

Organizing the assignment

The workshop had facilities to vacuum-form thermoplastic sheet, to bend and joint plastics including acrylic, to make moulds and construct electrical circuits.

Graphic and technical drawing facilities were easily accessed and included simple computer-aided design equipment (CAD).

The process of compiling the assignment was as follows:

- Flowcharting the process.
- Identifying which units and elements were covered in the process.
- Setting out the key tasks with supporting unit references.
- Writing the assignment to give the individual student the opportunity of a higher grading.
- Checking for core units.

Figure 8.2 illustrates what may be possible

7. Assignments linked to end tests: 'I do, I understand'

Where possible revision for the unit tests should relate to practical assignments. For example, in industrial practice, torch bodies will not be vacuum-formed but injection-moulded, except perhaps at the prototype stage. This could be an opportunity for students to be either taught about injection moulding or have it included in their assignment as an additional task to investigate. The limiting factor may be the resources available. A simple method used to anticipate the possible range of questions in the unit tests was to list from the syllabus the key words. For example Element 3.1. Range. Tools: trimming; fixing; cutting. One can cover these methods relating to perhaps, injection moulding or more manual methods.

There is no substitute for getting involved in the detail of the syllabus to understand the whole course and to generate ideas for creating assignments to ensure the coverage of the wide range of elements.

Delivering the programme

A student-centred approach

Based on experience from the pilot, it was decided to structure the course more tightly. It was important to bear in mind such points as the varying level and nature of students' study skills and their motivation for joining the course. It was also important to maximize their learning based on the assumption that some would only partially complete the course. It was considered unrealistic to expect all to finish the course or to complete all the units.

TASK	TASK DETAIL	UNIT/ELEMENT
Design problem	You are required to design & manufacture a prototype device for providing light in the dark. It should be battery powered.	1.1
Production constraints	Casing – vacuum formed. Simple switch. Use a PP3 battery.	1.1
Identify method of production		1.1
Developing potential designs		1.1
Evaluate manufacturing problems & constraints		1.1
Collect technical information on circuits		1.1
Flowchart key stages of manufacture		1.1
Complete simple working drawing		5.3
Present ideas to group		1.2
Prepare tools for manufacture		3.3
Production		3.3
Assembly		3.3
Finishing		3.3
Set quality standards		3.4
Test		3.4
Organise production		2.3
Additional – variations/extensions: Rewrite/redefine the problem. Established optimum production methods – using vacuum forming. Establish and organize 'workforce' to reduce costs. Present completed work with supporting advertising and presentation drawings.		

1. Mould for torch.
2. Mould split into top and bottom.
3. Top and Bottom vacuum formed. — trim
4. Casings finished. — locking tabs, mirror plastic, transparent acrylic plastic
5. Circuit built. — switch, battery clip, bulb holder, bulb
6. Completed assembly.

Figure 8.2 Product design and manufacture: a portable lighting device.

Thus one had to decide on the emphasis and essential objectives that should underpin the course. Although each unit and element has its own importance, it was felt that the student had to take with them from the course, key points that provided fundamental understanding of Manufacturing and the world of work. These key points were identified as follows:

- the importance of teamwork;
- the principle of an economic cost;
- the need to break down processes into their component parts;
- how a production line is organized;
- the importance of skill;
- the principle of division of labour;
- the need for continuity and persistence in the workplace and the key role of Health and Safety in the workplace;
- observation of factories at work.

The nature of GNVQ Manufacturing and the intake of students suggested that the emphasis of the course should be practical wherever possible. Main practical activities and case studies should relate to each other, emphasizing the key points that were selected. In addition, factory visits were seen as important as points of reference to reinforce manufacturing techniques and organization.

Three main manufacturing cycles were chosen:

1. Casting house number plates.
2. Making wooden pull-along toys for disabled children.
3. The design and manufacture of a torch.

In addition, there were activities such as making wooden jigsaws and acrylic display stands for small items.

To develop in-depth analysis skills, various items were examined. These included an electric jigsaw, electric scissors and a portable spot lamp. These were critically examined, sketches together with simple exploded drawings made, and then broken down into sub-assemblies. Discussions were held on possible simplification and better ways of manufacturing the same product. Discussion was recognized as an important learning resource.

Assuring quality

Although assignments were clearly laid out with evidence requirements and a standard in mind, assuring quality was the most difficult part of the course to administer. The method of assessment is well understood and requires the following: natural performance, simulations, projects and assignments, questioning, direct assessment

ment, candidate and peer reports, oral testing, written testing supported by observation or a completed artefact or product.

Using practical assignments it is clear that the product of the work provides individual or collective evidence that the course has been followed. The product can be examined to assess the standard. Equally the skills gained are inferred by outcome. What is more difficult to assess are the experience and understanding gained throughout. The end test may test some of the range but there must be built into the assignment a provision to review, discuss and test the student's experience. Notes can be taken on the student's natural performance throughout – for example, that Health and Safety considerations are being followed: Unit 4 Element 4.2. Identify the health and safety requirements for the individual and the workplace.

Unit tests

Unit tests were passed by all the students who finished the course. The optional choice was particularly welcome and students were confident in their understanding and answers compared with the pilot, where there was a higher degree of skill needed in comprehending the question and where students had to draw more on their own learning and experience. However, it is suspected that optional choice is perhaps not the best way for students to demonstrate their knowledge and understanding. Factory visits and practical examples provide students with experiences which contribute to the passing of the tests. It is suggested that Units 2, 3 and 4 are tackled early on in the course.

The teaching team

Based on the experience from the pilot it was decided that the course should be delivered by a number of teachers. The co-ordination of the delivery team is now acknowledged as being crucial to the provision of a quality course. The times to be assigned to the units and core, plus teacher allocation, were finalized as:

- Units 1 and 5 (4 hours; a Design and Technology teacher).
- Units 2 to 4 (5 hours; a Design and Technology teacher.
  Plus 3 hours; a specialist craftsperson).
- Unit 6 and part of Unit 4 (1 hour; a Science teacher).
- Core: Application of number (2 hours; a Maths teacher).
  Information Technology (1 hour; an IT teacher).
  Communication (1 hour; an English teacher).

The teaching of the core by specialist teachers proved to be unsatisfactory, although the IT specialist played a crucial role in the course. A significant part of the problem in teaching the core was related to the timetabling of only one hour per week. Similarly this created problems for the teaching of Material Science where poor student attendance resulted in gaps in the course.

The team was co-ordinated by a team member and the group met formally three times during the course. In addition, the team leader attended all the GNVQ meetings held in the school. Most of the co-ordinating work was therefore carried out informally. These arrangements proved only just adequate, experience having shown that the planning of the course with all team members present is crucial to its success.

Location of activities

All practical work was carried out in the workshop. In addition, Material Science (Unit 6) took place in a laboratory; Information Technology in an IT room provided with a network of computers; Design and graphics work in the Design and Technology rooms; all other core in normal classrooms.

Timetabling

As stated previously, most problems occurred when a teacher saw a student for only one hour in a week. This, in some cases, was exacerbated by poor student attendance. It was also difficult for the practical lab work to be repeated. Conversely, the most successful parts of the course were those that were held in blocks of two to three hours, thus enabling the student to complete work together with his team.

The students

The students were all male and most chose the course as they had rejected alternatives on offer. Many wished to progress in some form of practical activity as a career but not specifically in Manufacturing. Most were already friends. The group of 13 was split three ways in ability. Those with above average ability, those with adequate core skills and the remainder with poor core skills. Most had good social skills and could work well as members of a team.

The most successful had good motivation, whilst others with poor core skills struggled with the written part of the course.

Although one can argue that students should be selected on the basis of their core skills, for many these improved markedly throughout. Indeed, the group was characterized by its improved understanding of concepts and improved ability to analyse and present data by the end of the course.

Attendance and drop-out from the course

Although starting with 13 students, only five finished. Most left to enter some form of employment or to join the Armed Forces. The unexpected emphasis on paper evidence for many was a trial. However, for others it proved challenging and they made considerable effort towards the end of the course to ensure an up-to-date portfolio. Sporadic attendance by a few at crucial times – for example, during production runs – created problems for the others. Strategies need to be adopted to ensure continuity of attendance during group work.

Practical work

Casting

The planning of this project was linked to running it as a mini enterprise within the school. At the planning stage the number and capabilities of students were unknown.

The rationale for choosing casting in aluminium was as follows.

- It provided a realistic work situation, where teamwork was essential.
- There were clear Health and Safety considerations, and clear constraints on the production methods.
- There was a coherent progression from receipt of orders to the finishing and inspection of the finished article.
- There was skill acquisition and the opportunity to make improvements in production methods.
- Efficiency could be evaluated.
- There was the opportunity for work study.
- Quality of product was dependent on the skill of the pattern makers, and the casting team.
- As it was to be run as a mini enterprise, there was the need for business organization and customer services.
- We had good, modern casting facilities on site.

Time allocation

This was split into two: (a) skill acquisition; (b) production cycle. Linked to (a) was the time for obtaining orders from interested parties and the opportunity for organizing the associated paperwork.

Students were given the opportunity to design their own 'door plate', which could incorporate a motif of their choosing. They then completed simple working drawings and from this made patterns from MDF board. These were duly finished, enamelled and formed the mould for sand casting. Aluminium was melted and poured into the moulds. These were then finished by hand filing and painted appropriately. The operation was timed, discussed, flowcharted, and by agreement a team was established.

Mini enterprise

The team consisted of a production manager, a work study engineer who also maintained the machines in use and provided basic materials. These were designated 'the staff'.

The designated 'workers' were a sales team who also doubled as order processing and record-keeping clerks; a design team who took initial sketches from order sheets and converted them into simple working drawings; pattern makers who made the patterns for the casting operation; a casting team who under supervision from the teacher prepared the sand mould and poured the casting; an inspection team who accepted or rejected the rough casting and prepared it for the finishing process; and a finishing and packaging team who completed the process.

Experience of the production cycle

Ten hours were allocated, with the objective to manufacture the maximum quantity in that time. It also provided the opportunity for everyone to be usefully engaged in a productive activity. It was the 'staff' role to ensure this was managed and assured. Bottlenecks were to be avoided by transferring operators to the place of shortage.

At first everything functioned as expected and the students were quick to identify themselves in the role allocated. In theory it was possible to obtain six castings in one hour, in reality five were produced in two hours.

At one point the team forgot to withdraw the pattern before casting. This was quickly noticed at the point when the molten metal was poured. Work was stopped and the idea of using a checklist was suggested. Familiarity with a process, it seemed, was not a guarantee of quality.

The teacher who took the role of 'consultant' was forced to supervise the casting process more closely. This was found to interfere with his GNVQ role of assessor. Consequently, less time was allocated to the support of the 'staff' who by this time had established themselves in their roles. The following incident highlighted the problems caused by such a withdrawal of teacher involvement.

When production work was due to resume after the mid-morning break only the 'staff' arrived on time. On investigation, it was found that the 'workers' had resented their peers organizing them, felt undervalued and thus refused to co-operate. The situation was resolved through discussion and was used as an opportunity to discuss real industrial situations. Production was down but experiential learning was high.

Based on the pilot study, it was decided that job descriptions, together with forms such as order, stock, inspection and invoices would be designed by the group. These were created in IT core time and used during the production cycle. Although tasks were agreed and allocated and these were roughly designed by the students, this was not carried through in time for the production cycle. These problems were addressed and discussed with students who then realized that their absences caused problems with record keeping and identification of customer orders. The result was that the completeness of the project was compromised. Information was in danger of being fragmented.

To avoid this problem arising in the production cycle of the wooden toys the documentation was prepared beforehand. Although this approach of improved structure assisted the final evidence, it did take responsibility away from the group. Clearly there is a fine line to be drawn here. Future solutions suggested are to produce 'blank' templates so that students can obtain quick and effective results. This would also ensure that the emphasis is on production rather than on documentation.

Throughout the project, interest and motivation were high but teambuilding exercises prior to its start would have been useful. In addition, the selection of the 'production manager' is crucial. With the casting project he was ineffectual. Conversely, during the production of the toys, when no one was appointed, the group threw up its own leader who had a high work norm and good leadership qualities.

Wooden toys for disabled children

The rationale for this was as follows:

- The work had real value.
- There was the acquisition of skills.
- There were standards to be reached and maintained as only two designs were chosen.
- Efficiency could be evaluated clearly.
- There was an assembly element.

The timing was allocated in a similar way to the castings, namely skill acquisition and a production cycle. In addition simple work study was carried out and effective use of time was discussed.

Paperwork was prepared in advance and the teacher carefully organized work-study routines, where each part of the operation was closely supervised and timed.

Working on identical work and in close proximity created a greater feeling of teamwork.

The teacher worked closely with the team and improvements in materials and working methods were quickly identified. Because the team worked together, Health and Safety routines were observed by all, even when not directly involved.

Inspection, finishing and quality control

Inspection routines were established prior to the painting of the toys. However by the time the goods were painted, impetus was lost and the routine of painting, drying, finishing, repainting etc., resulted in a reduction in quality. However, plans to deliver the items to disabled children revived interest.

Again, many of these problems can be anticipated and this further emphasizes the importance of careful planning.

Links with Units 1 and 5

At the planning stage it was felt that it would be better that the main production cycles should not be dependent on prior work on designing. Design projects were set up independently with the units being self-contained wherever possible. However, some graphic and presentation work was completed after the castings were completed. This rationale was adopted because of the problems of timing. It was necessary to get the casting production going quickly. In addition students might experience variations on a theme at the expense of original learning opportunities.

However, in the design and manufacture of the torch, integration was possible.

The design and manufacture of a torch

This assignment has already been touched upon, but basically the students, in addition to designing and making the outer casing, had to build a simple electrical circuit. Like other projects, skill and understanding through the production process were seen as the key.

Sub-assemblies and assemblies were discussed, the order of production flowcharted, and finally the torches were manufactured. A 'brief' was created and students had to design and manufacture a torch within the constraints of that brief, i.e. to a set manufacturing method using vacuum forming, styrene and acrylic plastics, to build a simple electrical circuit with light holders, bulbs, battery connectors and switches.

The timing of the manufacture of this product was late in the course and so a minimum production run using individual patterns for moulding was organized.

The success of this project was partly based on the choice of components and manufacturing techniques which were easy to use and organize. One can see that more complex electronic circuits, perhaps ones that flash, can provide a more varied learning situation with opportunity for testing, inspection and the use of experimental production teams.

Information Technology and the use of spreadsheets

Spreadsheet use was taught under Information Technology (IT). However, templates previously set up for each production cycle gave the opportunity to extrapolate figures and ask 'what if' questions. These were useful for costing and could be used for production planning once each component part or sub-assembly had been established.

In future, spreadsheets should be used whenever possible, with advance planning giving maximum benefit.

Short, design and make, case studies

Designing and making a simple jigsaw and acrylic display stands for small items give the opportunity for pairs of students to work together to carry out some simple work study, which can then be documented, discussed and worked upon. This has perhaps greatest potential when linked with simple spreadsheets which can have pre-costed overheads etc. set as standard.

Examination of existing products

These acted as 'practical case studies' where items were disassembled, sketched and components identified.

The portable spotlight

Having already covered the theory of various manufacturing techniques – one example being injection moulding – the types of plastics were identified and, using 'guestimates' of costs, decisions were made concerning either purchase from outside or in-house manufacture. Standard components such as screws, nuts, bolts, and springs were identified.

Having identified all the components, one could establish the order of assembly from sub-assemblies to final assembly. Estimates were made as to the timing of these operations. Again this can be extrapolated on spreadsheets.

Factory visits

A number of industrial facilities were visited, each with its own specific production problems. They were:

- a caravan factory;
- a car assembly plant;
- a plant extruding aluminium window frames;
- a yoghurt factory;
- a sewerage works.

The caravan factory

Prior to the visit, a video on the history of the mobile home introduced the topic and a variety of production methods were presented from archive film. Based on this, students had to design a caravan, identifying the main sub-assemblies. Using Lego they designed a layout of what they considered to be the order of production.

It was found that Lego allowed students to explore and discuss production layouts quickly, as it gave easy access to three-dimensional modelling.

A list of questions was compiled from their own investigations prior to the factory visit. Although some of their ideas were correct, the visit showed them many innovative production techniques and materials. Batch production was predominant, with panels being built in batches on specific jigs using staple guns. The emphasis on speed of production was evident in what is still a labour-intensive assembly method.

After the visit, the checklist was reviewed and students prepared a report on their findings.

Motor vehicle assembly

The contrasts with the caravan factory were obvious. The emphasis was high-tech, capital intensive, with the use of robots in presses and assembly.

Aluminium extrusion

The mix of 1970s technology with more recent innovations was evident. The large amount of money tied up in stock was noted. The high-tech method of production and finishing the extruded material contrasted with the labour-intensive, skilled, window fabrication.

Health and Safety requirements were conscientiously adhered to in this plant.

Yoghurt manufacture

Health and hygiene requirements were clearly a high priority here and were characterized by the special clothing required. Automation was used in a process geared to long production runs. Plant that manufactured the plastic containers just prior to filling contrasted with that which filled bought-in containers which presented a security risk of contamination at source or during transit.

Sewerage plant

Element 4.3: Identify the environmental effects of production processes.

To support Unit 4, a sewerage plant was visited, where all manner of liquids were handled successfully. Again this experience assisted the learning.

The more varied the visits that can be arranged, the more understanding that can be related to practical projects. This contrasted with the students' three weeks' work experience.

Work experience

It is the school's policy to arrange three weeks' work experience and this is organized through a local agency. The usefulness of the work experience to the course was evident through subsequent discussion of the group's individual and collective experience. Two students worked in a small factory which blister-packs products for major manufacturers. All aspects of the problems relating to a small business were in evidence. Teamwork, boredom, bonuses, health and safety, division of labour, technical problems, quality, deadlines, lead-times and stock control. Compare this with the experience of students who worked in a maintenance workshop of a chemical plant where health and safety dominated and few demands were made on the student. Further, compare this with the engineering firm where skilled operators used centre lathes seemingly without supervision or direction and where the managing director was known as the 'dark horse', never being seen in daylight hours! Work experience, carefully chosen, must add to the quality of the course.

Although students had to observe and report on their work experience, many found it difficult to make sense of it in 'manufacturing terms' without having first reviewed it in class. Therefore, it is possibly unwise to include their work experience in specific elements of the units.

Looking forward: a review

The GNVQ Manufacturing syllabus is written in a general way and this gives the flexibility for centres to organize the course in line with their own facilities. However, it demands detailed teacher planning to ensure that students know exactly, at each stage, what is required from them in terms of evidence. Each identifiable part of the syllabus must produce evidence which shows coverage.

There are some main issues that remain crucial to the success of GNVQ Manufacturing. These are the students, the planning and resourcing of the course, the commitment of the delivery staff and the relevance of the course to the students.

With the benefit of hindsight one can see the pitfalls. The emphasis on this review is therefore to forward-think in order to maximize the situation in future whilst recognizing that we do not have an 'ideal' world.

The students

It is tempting to assert that for some students the Intermediate level course was too difficult as their core skills were poor. This was evident in the standard of their documentary evidence. This suggests that there should be some level of selection based on core skills prior to acceptance on the programme. Our experience suggests otherwise. Students who on enrolment had low core skills but had high motivation and attended well, clearly benefited from the course. Motivation and interest was the key.

Assessment

Assessment should perhaps focus on the potential of students and the support they will need to ensure that potential's realization, not on current level of core-skill competence. Experience demonstrated that students with low motivation and interest failed to perform consistently in teamworking, and were more likely to have sporadic attendance and fail to present the completed assignment on time. As an emphasis was made on teambuilding, their poor performance affected the group's overall work ethic.

It is important therefore that staff regularly review student work in all areas and where appropriate discuss the relevance of the course with the student. Steps need to be taken to ensure that others are not hindered by these students' lack of performance.

The planning and resourcing of the course

A course co-ordinator must be appointed and he/she must be committed to developing the course and ensuring its resourcing. It is desirable that in the early stages the course co-ordinator is actively involved in the delivery of units and understands the processes and problems likely to be encountered. Adequate time for planning must be allocated, with regular monthly review meetings – the latter being designed to review and amend the course where necessary and to review student progress and attainment. The desirability of block timetabling has already been touched upon.

The diversity of the manufacturing industry presented both problems and opportunities for the delivery staff. Fortunately our school has good industrial links and we can organize visits linked to coursework. Videos used selectively can give relevance and reality to an issue. For example, the choice of caravan manufacture as a manufacturing process resulted from the availability of a video.

In preparing the course it was found that some considerable effort has to be made in obtaining relevant manufacturing information. A chapter on planning came from one source whilst information on total quality management was gained from another. The provision of an appropriate study resource for students to gather information was therefore problematic. Hence the need for high contact time. However, issues like Health and Safety are now well documented and students were able to glean relevant information and supporting documentation from readily available publications. Their theoretical knowledge was reinforced by their own practical experience and factory visits/work experience.

Staff involvement and commitment

Students have a degree of choice in attending school or a college of further education. Professionals have a commitment to creating opportunities for young people at this important and formative time of their development. A relevant and quality course should therefore attract students and be successful. However, staff need a good framework to work within and provided problems are identified early steps can be taken to improve the situation. Staff updating and continual professional development in schools are also important where relevant industrial experience may be sparse.

Relevance

Many of the issues covered in GNVQ Manufacturing are touched upon in a Business Studies course and vice versa. However, the practical processes of designing to need, prototyping, costing, teamworking and manufacturing consistently to a specification, evolving new methods of manufacture, are best taught through a practical course. It is broader than a skill-based NVQ but can give the student that developing feeling of competence through understanding. Responding to the challenge of teamworking, communicating ideas, and problem-solving in real situations with real consequences provides students with a clearer insight into the world of work. Linked with industry, and relevant work experience, the course clearly has the potential to prepare young people more thoroughly for the transition to employment or further studies.

PART THREE Progression

Chapter 9

JILL JOHNSON # Higher Education and Employment

GNVQ is a qualification which is promoted as being suitable for progression to both employment and higher studies. Within any one group of students there may be individuals with very different needs, and it will be necessary to achieve a balance which as far as possible enables individual students to achieve their aims.

The decisions the students need to make post-16 are possibly the most important ones of their lives. They have a number of options open, depending on the type of school they have attended and on their immediate aims and objectives. Approximately 90 per cent of 16-year-olds will continue either with their studies or go into training, and a large proportion of these will decide that the vocational route (and GNVQ or NVQ are the main options available) is best suited for them.

The vocational route, and particularly GNVQs, will probably be the least familiar to 16-year-olds. Therefore, careful consideration must be given to the way information about GNVQ is presented. The progression routes available need to be clearly identified, the various pathways made clear, and the differences between alternative qualifications at the same level explained. Guidance to individuals on the modes of study and assessment best suited to them is required; for instance, students who have been more successful with the coursework components of GCSE than with the externally examined components may well find the continuous assessment of GNVQ more to their liking, and feel that it will provide them with a greater chance of successful completion. On the other hand, there is evidence that potential A-level students are choosing to undertake Advanced GNVQ because they recognize the advantages of the opportunities for active and autonomous learning, and the development of skills which are so necessary for success in their future careers.

The main message for teachers and tutors is that because GNVQ is so new, it has not yet attained the recognition of qualifications which are better known and understood; it therefore needs to be carefully explained to students, parents and employers, and the many advantages it has need to be highlighted (disadvantages will also need to be touched on!).

What therefore can be done?

Planning for progression

Firstly, planning needs to be undertaken both by institutions, teachers and lecturers and individual students. The information provided before students embark on a GNVQ programme requires special attention, as does the guidance which is given to individuals prior to and on entry. Issues to be addressed include:

1. Guidance during Years 10 and 11.
2. The interview.
3. Design of GNVQ programmes.
4. The induction programme.

1. Guidance during Years 10 and 11

This will be provided in a number of ways:

- through the Careers Service;
- through careers staff within schools;
- work shadowing;
- talks from employers;
- talks by schools liaison staff at sixth form colleges, and colleges of further education.

The Morrisby Profiles are useful in the counselling process as they identify possible career routes available based on an individual's strengths in a number of different areas. These could help to decide whether the GNVQ route is most appropriate.

The action plans within the Record of Achievement are particularly important in getting individual students to think about their future plans, and to encourage them to investigate possible progression routes for the future.

2. The interview

If progression post-16 is to be to a sixth-form college or college of further education, selection to GNVQ programmes will probably be carried out by interview. Centres are, of course, bound by the open access policy of the GNVQ. One of the features of a quality programme is the manner in which the interviewing process is conducted. It needs to be structured, but lively, interesting and informative. The use of videos, displays of current students' work, photographs of activities undertaken on the programme, etc., help to make the occasion enjoyable rather than daunting. Parent participation should be encouraged wherever possible. The interview also provides the opportunity for diagnostic tasks to be set, in order to enable individual students, their parents, and tutors, to determine the most appropriate GNVQ level. On the other hand, if progression is within the same institution, an extension of the guidance and counselling process above will be the most likely procedure.

This stage is particularly important for teachers and tutors as it provides an opportunity to ascertain the likely aspirations of the incoming group of GNVQ students. At this stage, individuals need to be encouraged to identify what their present intentions are with regard to progression post-GNVQ, recognizing of course that these intentions may well change. This process links closely with the next point.

3. Design of GNVQ programmes

Opportunities for progression could be influenced to a significant extent by the rationale behind the manner in which teachers and lecturers design the programmes to be delivered. This is especially true for Advanced GNVQ where the overall programme needs to be designed in such a way that students are not denied progression opportunities at a future date.

GNVQ has now been delivered in schools and colleges for the past two years, and other chapters of this publication provide details of the experiences of those involved. Hopefully lessons can be learned from the suggestions and advice given.

In brief, issues to be considered include:

(a) The need to meet the requirements for future progression, whether to employment or higher studies, of as many students as possible.
(b) Knowledge of these requirements. If a student is progressing to higher education from an Advanced GNVQ, universities and colleges may have identified specific units which need to be achieved in order for that student to be considered for a programme.

(c) If a centre delivering GNVQ does not have the necessary resources in order to make available the necessary optional or additional units to meet individual requirements, it may be necessary to investigate whether or not it is possible to collaborate with another school or college in order to give as wide a choice as possible to students.

(d) The integration of core skills into the mandatory and optional units. Centres with more experience of delivering GNVQ are clearly identifying the opportunities for assessment of the core-skill units within the context of the vocational area. It could be that core skills will be the key to progression opportunities in the future, and careful consideration needs to be given to the opportunities provided for assessment.

(e) The additionality which is made available. Decisions need to be made about the desirability or otherwise of offering the basic GNVQ, or whether it should be supplemented with other units, qualifications or modules.

The number of units to be made available within a programme also needs to be decided. Some universities are insisting that for progression to a degree programme it is necessary for an Advanced GNVQ student to have achieved 18 units plus the three mandatory core-skill units. However, others have recognized the enormity of this task and feel that 15 units, perhaps more carefully chosen, is more appropriate.

The desirability or otherwise, and of course the feasibility from the centre point of view, of providing the opportunity to achieve the three non-mandatory core-skill units also need to be addressed, particularly because these three skills will be so important to individuals for their future success, whether they progress to employment or to further studies.

(f) The order in which the units are delivered needs to be decided. The method of grading needs to be considered; as grading is only attached to mandatory units and optional units, should these units be delivered at the beginning or more towards the end of the programme? Students need the opportunity to develop these skills throughout a GNVQ programme, and it may well be unrealistic to front-load the assessed units and expect young people to provide evidence towards the higher grades straight away.

(g) Should a utilized, a semi-integrated, or a fully-integrated approach be adopted? This issue is well debated in the vocational chapters.

(h) What is the role of work experience/placement/shadowing in the programme? Links with local employers can provide the opportunity for students to impress within the workplace and from this possibly obtain an offer of employment. Work experience (particularly a good report from an employer) may also provide evidence towards some of the GNVQ criteria. In some instances, working for a number of years may be a specific requirement in order to progress to certain award routes at university.

(i) How should the grading criteria be introduced? Some of the strands of the grading themes are higher-order skills and need firstly to be taught, and then developed over a period of time, in order to enable students to achieve the Merit and Distinction grades. When designing delivery, it may therefore be better to introduce the 'easier' skills of information seeking, followed a few assessments later by an introduction to the process of action planning, rather than expecting students to understand the implications of all the grading themes from Assessment No. 1. This approach could result in higher grades being achieved which will enhance opportunities for progression.

4. The induction programme

Time should be made available to discuss with students their future aspirations, and to provide guidance on the best way forward and the best units and/or qualifications to study.

It is not too soon to encourage those Advanced GNVQ students who plan to progress to higher education, to use library or Careers Service facilities, or to use the UCAS Handbook to get ideas of possible progression award routes. This can be followed up in subsequent tutorials by getting students to send off for university prospectuses.

Induction can be used to give tasters of different qualifications available so that students experience various kinds of study before actually embarking upon it. Students could undertake short periods of work shadowing to provide ideas for future employment.

Working towards progression

Students who determine aims and objectives for the future are more likely to be successful than the ones who undertake the GNVQ programme, making unit choices which are convenient at the time, and without real thought for what they are going to be doing on completion. However, a GNVQ is designed to be a broad-based qualification, and will prepare students for a number of choices for the future. A large number of 16- and 17-year-olds in particular, do not have clear progression objectives at the start of a programme. These students will possibly require a greater degree of guidance than those who have clearly identified the requirements of their chosen progression route.

It is important that the students are encouraged to think about their aspirations from the start of the programme. Teachers and lecturers therefore need to build into the design the opportunity for further preparation towards either employment or further study.

This can be done in a number of ways:

1. The tutorial
2. Involvement of industry.
3. Preparation for higher education.
4. Preparation for employment.

1. The tutorial

Having provided the opportunity for identification of the medium-term aims of your student on entry to the programme, regular reviews need to take place to check that the student is on course.

These reviews need to take into account the progress being made within the qualification. If it becomes apparent that the sights which an individual has set are unrealistic, that person will need counselling on other options available. However, a student may make better-than-expected progress and may need to be encouraged to aim higher. Factors such as the number of units which need to be achieved, the grade which is prerequisite of certain progression routes, performance in the core-skill units, success or otherwise in the unit tests and in meeting the necessary performance criteria, all need to be monitored. The grade profile will also need to be considered.

One-to-one reviews need to take place at least termly, but some students may need more frequent help.

2. Involvement of industry

Opportunities for work shadowing, or for meeting performance criteria whilst in the workplace, can give students a valuable insight into different types of work settings and this may help to crystallize their plans.

Alternatively, you may wish to get representatives from the different types of business operating within the vocational area to give talks, to conduct interviews, to act as members of a panel to which oral presentations are made, to allow students to conduct research within their organizations, or to provide specific information to prepare for assessments.

The Education Business Partnerships also have an important role in facilitating links between business organizations and education establishments, and hopefully will play a more central role in the delivery of vocational qualifications in the future.

Similarly, if students have an opportunity to participate in the Business Mentoring Scheme, this can develop job skills for the future, and further cultivate business/education links.

All these provide valuable sources of information for students and as GNVQs are *vocational* qualifications it is unrealistic to deliver them without providing the opportunity for students to experience industry in some form or other, albeit briefly.

3. Preparation for higher education

This section obviously only applies to those Advanced GNVQ students wishing to progress to university or college of higher education in order to undertake a first degree, a HND, or the less popular DipHE course.

It has already been stated that it is a good idea to get students to start to plan for progression to HE at induction. However, proper preparation will need to start in earnest in about February of the first year of the programme (assuming most Advanced GNVQs are achieved over a two-year period). The following paragraphs provide brief information on some of the relevant sources of data available.

The UCAS (Universities and Colleges Admissions Service) Handbook

This is an excellent starting point to give students an idea of the range of options available. The index is particularly useful as it refers the user to alternative options within the same broad subject area, and can therefore identify options which would not otherwise have been considered. It also provides details of combinations of subjects it is possible to study. However, it does not give detailed information on individual award routes, merely listing those which are available at individual Higher Education Institutions.

University and college prospectuses

These provide more detailed information on the structure of courses available, and on the institution concerned. They give some information on entry requirements for individual award routes, but this is usually limited to specified A level or BTEC grades, or number of A-level points required, together with an indication of the required performance at GCSE. Many entries in the 1995 prospectuses now refer to Advanced GNVQ, and the requirements of students progressing from this entry route. Remember though that a prospectus will give an institution's view of what is offered in line with their mission statement. Good GNVQ students will of course be aware of this through the development of the skill of information handling!

The student prospectus service

Up to ten prospectuses can be obtained from a list of 203 HEIs, for the cost of the phone call. The service uses a recorded message which is charged at 39 or 49 pence per minute. The full call time is 5 minutes at a cost of £2.45. This service is provided by Official Mailing Services Limited, and is a convenient way for students to obtain the prospectuses they wish to peruse. Delivery is promised within about a week, but in practice this can take a little longer.

University and College Entrance – the Official Guide

This weighty tome, published by UCAS, contains detailed information on all courses available at HEIs within the UCAS system, together with entry requirements.

ECCTIS 2000

The UCAS database, available in many schools and colleges on CD-ROM, contains the updated version of the *UCAS Handbook*, and enables students to search under a number of different fields for information on individual award routes. It provides a good amount of detail; particularly useful is the number of applications and number of acceptances provided for many courses, and content of the different components of the course. It also lists the accepted entry routes, and information on Advanced GNVQ is now included for some institutions and some award routes.

The Morrisby Organization Vocational Guidance Service

A Guidance Report is provided to many students in schools in Year 11 and is intended to get individuals to think about their future. It concentrates on the abilities and aspirations of each person, and identifies strengths and potential. It then identifies the options available, and this section can usefully be used in conjunction with the sources of information dealt with above to try to find higher education programmes which will match the strengths of that person.

A further service, Course Finder 2000, is specifically geared to higher education courses.

Centigrade

This is a service at present offered jointly by UCAS and Cambridge Occupational Analysts Limited (COA) on payment of a fee of £9.50. Centigrade attempts to identify the types of course an individual would like to undertake, and to identify those HEIs in which an individual will flourish. After a short introduction, it provides an 'Interest Profile' which gives details of the higher education interest areas, the interest level as a percentage, the overall match as a percentage, and the relevant subjects that interest area requires. The subsequent section provides 'Your Course Selection' and lists the courses and locations which match with the individual's interest level and academic level. This is followed by a useful section including Course Analysis Forms and Action Plan together with examples of how the necessary planning can be undertaken. Finally, there are some general sections providing UCAS Course Codes, Maps, and Abbreviations and Reference Sources.

Centigrade is especially helpful for students who do not have a clear idea of the options available to them. It is also a useful starting point for matching individuals' achievements with the requirements of individual courses. Used in conjunction with the Morrisby Profiles it can provide a useful focus for guidance provided in tutorials.

Records of Achievement

The experience of looking forward in a purposeful manner is one of the qualities which is sought by admissions tutors, although the document is rarely fully examined by them.

However, Records of Achievement will encourage students to think through the options available to them more clearly. Thus, they will make more informed choices, construct a better and more structured personal statement, and present themselves more effect- ively if called to interview.

Commercial publications

There are a number of these available and some are held in school and college libraries, specifically the Careers Section. One of the most amusing is *PUSH – The Polytechnic & University Student's Handbook*. It is written very much with young people in mind and is intended as supplementary information to some of the more official publications already discussed. It aims to give material on what young people really want to know, not the boring stuff on course codes, etc.! The kind of information provided is where to go for the social life, the position regarding accommodation, the 'real feel' of the institution and location. *PUSH 95* is compiled by J. and B. Rich and costs £9.95, although it can be available at a discount in some instances. It is obtainable through any bookshop.

Other publications include:

(a) *Potter Guide to HE* – this gives general information to start, and then lists universities within regions, giving details on the campus, on the city/town, and on 'escape routes' (where to go in the surrounding area).
(b) *Degree Course Guides* – once again general details are provided, but also included is information on the style and content of the courses, teaching and assessment methods, transfer between courses, selection procedures and entrance requirements, gra- duate outlook, etc.
(c) *Compendium of HE* – lists universities in alphabetical order but under broad headings, e.g. Arts, Sciences, etc.

Student fairs

These are provided by various organizations and give students general information about what is on offer from HEIs and employers. For those students wishing to investigate the possibility of attending a university in another member state of the European Community, an annual fair is held in Brussels in February. Many UK HEIs are also represented there.

Open days and pre-taster courses

Information on many of those available is published by UCAS in booklet form, and schools and colleges will also receive invitations from HEIs direct, particularly those within the local area.

This is a valuable opportunity for students to visit an institution, and possibly a new location, and to see for themselves what a university or college is really like. Some Open Days are general in nature, others are specifically aimed at certain areas, e.g. Science. Although the days are arranged by staff within the institution itself, there is nearly always the opportunity to gain a different perspective by talking to current students.

Such days could also be very helpful for GNVQ students to talk to staff at the HEI concerned to ascertain if the qualification is acceptable to the admissions tutor for specific award routes in which they might be interested.

Compacts

There is no doubt that compacts are an important development of the past few years. They offer above all a far more seamless progression into higher education than the barrier the admissions process has proved to be for many applicants in the past. The relationship of all those involved in the FE/HE interface is of crucial importance to young people, and the growth in local links has already benefited many potential applicants.

Generally, entry requirements for most award routes available within certain HEIs are negotiated with local schools and colleges.

Representatives from universities and colleges of higher education are closely involved in the planning process which needs to be undertaken as preparation for entry to HE.

The principal benefit to students is that they know more explicitly the achievements needed for successful progression. Frequently, local compact goals are set which include academic and extracurricular achievement, and 'points' are negotiated with further education providers to give an indication to students of the necessary requirements. Points may often be given for qualifications, qualities and achievements not currently recognized within the A-level points system. Due to the close links of the organizations involved, a mutual understanding of what one is offering, and of what the other is seeking, is developed. Frequently the 'points score' for an applicant from a compact partner is substantially less than for those applying through the more traditional route.

Some compacts have been devised specifically to recruit applicants from non-traditional qualification routes, or from backgrounds where there is no history of progression into higher education. This can benefit the Advanced GNVQ student.

Guidelines on compacts have been produced by the Further Education Unit in collaboration with the GATE Project.

FE/HE partnerships

Like compacts, this is currently a fast-developing strategy for increasing the participation rate within higher education. With partnerships part or the whole of a HND or degree programme is delivered within a further education institution with validation of the award by the partner university.

To date it is known that some arrangements between partner institutions have been made for progression from Advanced GNVQ, but numbers of students involved are small. Presumably as the qualification gains a greater number of candidates, arrangements will be made for increased progression via this mechanism. Again, as with compacts the barriers of the admissions process are removed, much to the benefit of the individual student; in most instances it is not necessary to go through the formal admissions system.

Admissions tutors or staff from central admissions offices

The GNVQ student should be encouraged to contact the admissions tutors for the award routes in which they are interested to ascertain the acceptability of their qualification. This is not always easy, but if left until the time of actual application, it could be too late to negotiate the incorporation into the programme of any particular units which are required.

In addition, remember to check what achievement is required at Key Stage 4. Many HEIs will request attainment of GCSE Maths and English at Grade C or above. If some of your students have progressed from, say, Intermediate to Advanced level GNVQ, they may not have these achievements. It may therefore be necessary to negotiate acceptance of the GNVQ core skills of Communication and/or Application of Number as alternatives if this is possible. Comparisons of these areas are presently taking place.

There may also be specific requirements set by professional bodies associated with some awards. Students and tutors need to be aware of this, although these should be clearly specified in the prospectus.

4. Preparation for employment

Unfortunately, there has not been as much research undertaken into progression by GNVQ students into employment. There is therefore currently a dearth of information available. Those statistics available do tend to show that approximately 50 per cent of students achieving GNVQ at any of the three levels will probably wish to progress into the job market, rather than into further studies. It is important therefore that this section of students is not neglected.

GNVQ does provide an extremely valuable chance to bring students into contact with employers. There is no doubt that these students can stand a far better chance of being offered employment than those making a 'sight-unseen' application. GNVQ, like BTEC courses before, also provides opportunities for students to host events and displays and to invite employers to see and recognize their achievements.

Information on employment opportunities can also of course be obtained from the usual sources: the Careers Service, professional bodies, the local and national press, etc.

Applying for progression

This section concentrates on applications to higher education, mainly because more information is available on progression to this route than to the employment route. Many of the comments made, however, may equally refer to both routes. Inevitably, the section also concentrates on progression from Advanced GNVQ, rather from the other levels.

Unless progression to higher education is through a partnership scheme, preparations to complete the UCAS form should be well under way by the start of Year 2. There is considerable evidence to suggest that the early bird catches the worm, and although applications sent to UCAS up to 15 December are in theory treated equally, in practice places for popular award routes may be filled before that date. It is important to realize that because GNVQ is still relatively unknown and misunderstood by some admissions tutors, extra effort needs to be made to ensure that the students stand as great a chance of success as possible. It is perhaps unfortunate that the first cohort of Advanced GNVQ students applying to higher education came at a time of contraction of numbers within that sector. Generally speaking though, applications from this first cohort have been favourably received by universities and colleges of higher education, and few applicants have been left without an offer. This has been the result of a considerable expenditure of time and energy by representatives from the further education sector. Such efforts will need to continue until Advanced GNVQ is better known by higher education institutions and probably when they have had the chance to track the performance of GNVQ students currently entering.

Which HEIs should GNVQ applicants choose?

Obviously, those where local links have been forged, whether formal or informal will be the best bet. It is also more likely that institutions which previously accepted applicants from the BTEC National Diploma route will wish to consider applications from GNVQ students. However, much work to promote GNVQ, and to inform HEIs about it, is taking place and during the 1994 round of applications offers were received by Advanced GNVQ students from universities which might not previously have considered applicants from the vocational route. It also depends of course on whether an admissions tutor is *selecting* or *recruiting* applicants to his/her programme.

The GATE database, currently available in paper form but available on computer disk shortly, gives information as to whether or not Advanced GNVQ is acceptable, and the position on interview and conditions. However, at present the information relates to the institution as a whole and not to individual award routes.

The GATE Project has produced an analysis of the experiences of the first phase Advanced GNVQ students who applied for higher education courses. The Project is also providing appropriate higher education staff development activities and organizing curriculum network groups at which issues are discussed and students' portfolios inspected.

Choice of programme

Analysis of applicants from the first cohort of Advanced GNVQ students shows that the vast majority of them have applied to progress to programmes which are fairly closely connected with the vocational area in which they studied for their GNVQ.

There is, however, no real reason why GNVQ students should be limited to progression within a narrow vocational area, and opportunities may be lost by having a somewhat blinkered view of the options available. Advanced GNVQ students should be encouraged to investigate other possibilities before committing themselves, and indeed some admissions tutors are expressing the view that they would welcome, for example, applications from students in GNVQ

Business to a Valuers or Computer Studies course. Other admissions tutors have indicated that they would prefer applications from outside the vocational area, especially as there may be some overlap between what is delivered in the Advanced GNVQ and what is delivered, particularly in the first year, at HE. On the other hand, there may well be specific requirements of achievement in a particular area.

If the planning and preparation suggested earlier in this chapter have occurred, by the time it is necessary to submit an application Advanced GNVQ students should have a clear idea of what is available to them, and what it is they wish to undertake.

Matching student to programme

It is now recognized that it is desirable to persuade HEIs to provide in far greater detail than previously, explicit details of the criteria which are used in order to determine whether an applicant will be taken on to a chosen award route. Work has started with a very limited number of institutions to enable this to be done, and useful progress is being made between a small number of other institutions on a more informal basis.

There is informal evidence to suggest that as many as 40 per cent of students currently studying within higher education feel that they have made the wrong choice of award route. It is often difficult to change track (often because of funding constraints) once a programme has been started, although the development of modularization in HE is obviating this problem to some extent.

It is therefore essential for the student and their advisers to have as much detail as possible as to whether or not there is a match between the achievements and qualities of the student and those being sought by the admission tutors involved.

Special efforts need to be made to ensure that the GNVQ student can present evidence to HEIs of the necessary depth and breadth of knowledge, of development of skills which are an inherent part of GNVQ, and of the qualities which are needed for successful progression.

Completion of the UCAS form

It goes without saying that the instructions for completion of the form should be followed carefully, and these do include details on GNVQ.

Section 7B is particularly problematic for GNVQ applicants as there is often insufficient room to detail the units which have been, or are going to be, achieved, particularly if the student is working towards 18 vocational units and three or more core-skill units. A possible solution is to complete the initial details, and then to ignore the columns given, and to write across the whole page giving details of units under the four headings of Mandatory, Optional, Core Skill, and Additionality. The latter area will need careful thought if this includes qualifications other than units from within the specific vocational area. Remember to include a '(c)' for those units which have already been completed. If centres have decided to arrange for unit accreditation as the qualification has proceeded, then these units could of course be included in Section 7A, but this could perhaps be even more confusing for admissions tutors!

The Personal Statement needs to be reflective as well as informative. It needs to identify and link the wealth of evidence which is part and parcel of the GNVQ with short-, medium- and long-term aspirations. Admissions tutors may not know how rigorous and challenging the GNVQ programme has been, how the student has taken responsibility for his/her own learning to the extent reflected by the grade achieved, and how autonomous learning skills have been developed. The core-skill units are particularly important; the non-mandatory ones possibly even more so than those which are part of the qualification. It is known that admissions tutors are looking for evidence of the ability to highlight achievement through experience; it is therefore not a good idea merely to describe what has been achieved.

Some of these issues can be addressed in the reference section, although care should be taken that duplication of information should not occur. As a teacher or tutor you must try to convince the HEIs to which application has been made that your student from the GNVQ route is truly worth consideration. You can match the qualities and skills which are developed through achievement of the qualification with what you think the admissions tutors are seeking.

Post application

Some centres involved with applications in the 1994 round have tried to provide additional information on GNVQ once the UCAS number has been received, but unfortunately this has often not reached the destination for which it was intended. Staff from many FEIs have become personally involved in discussions with admissions tutors to try to convince them of the worth of the applicant through the GNVQ route. Offers have tended to come rather later than expected for the GNVQ applicants, possibly because HEIs knew comparatively little of the nature of the qualification. Other HEIs have assumed that GNVQ is a replacement for BTEC National Diplomas, and if these have been acceptable in the past then GNVQ has tended to be now. However, it is evident that there is still a lack of proper understanding within HE about the nature of GNVQ, and this is exacerbated by criticisms from some quarters. Teachers and lecturers will still therefore need to keep a watch on the progress of applications and possibly liaise directly with HEIs on their students' behalf.

The portfolio of evidence

This contains much of the evidence (e.g. organizational ability, the breadth and/or depth of knowledge, of communication skills) that admissions tutors would like, but the bulk involved makes them inaccessible. Students could, however, take examples of work if asked to attend for interview, together with their Record of Achievement if available.

Conclusion

There are undoubtedly opportunities for progression from GNVQ, both into employment and into higher education. At present, however, much still needs to be done to inform employers and staff within higher education of the nature of a GNVQ and the opportunities it presents for individuals – not only to gain knowledge and understanding of a vocational area but also to develop skills which will lead to a greater chance of success in the future.

Different types of communication skills are assessed within a GNVQ, use is made of information technology, and mathematical techniques are *applied* within the context of a programme area: these are what employers and admissions tutors say they are looking for, and these are only the mandatory core-skill units, so only a taster of more to come from a GNVQ.

In addition, there is the opportunity to provide evidence and of being assessed in three further skills: those of working with others, managing one's own learning, and problem-solving; again these are achieved within a specific context, and are not abstract and isolated.

There is also the wealth of evidence generated from the application of the grading themes, unique to GNVQ.

Lastly, there are the other qualities which are developed by undertaking a GNVQ: motivation, commitment, meeting deadlines, coping with challenges, organization, and many more.

With proper planning and preparation on the part of teachers and lecturers our GNVQ students can be equipped to progress from their qualification with skills which will serve them well for the rest of their careers. We have a duty to these students to make sure that all the relevant organizations, and the people within them, are aware of these achievements, and how GNVQ students can contribute with confidence to the success of the institutions to which they progress.

Appendix

Contact names and telephone numbers for organizations referred to in this publication:

1. **Education Business Partnerships**
   These are organized regionally by the Training and Enterprise Councils. For information contact your local TEC.

2. **Business Monitoring Scheme**
   This is a new scheme offering one-to-one help for another person to learn. Again contact your local TEC for more information.

3. **The Student Prospectus Service**
   For information and copies of up to ten selected prospectuses, call the Student Line on 0891 717259. The service is offered by Official Mailing Services Limited, 6 Bushey Hall Road, Bushey, Herts WD2 2EA, and Lissadel Street, Salford M6 6FZ.

4. ***University and College Entrance – The Official Guide 1995***
   Copies are available either direct from Sheed & Ward Ltd, 14 Coopers Row, London EC3N 2BH, Tel. 0171 702 9799, or from bookshops.
   UK Price £12, plus £3 p. & p.

5. **Universities & Colleges Admissions Service**
   Fulton House, Jessop Avenue, Cheltenham, Gloucestershire GL50 3SH. Main Office: Tel. 01242 222 444; General Enquiries: Tel. 01242 227788.

6. **ECCTIS 2000**
   Contact UCAS, see above.
   Educational subscription is £180 for one year.

7. **Morrisby Organization Vocational Guidance Service**
   For further information Tel. 0144 268645.

8. **Centigrade**
   Contact: Cambridge Occupational Analysts Limited, Tel. 01362 688722.

9. **GATE Project**
   Academic Services & Development Department, UCAS, 1st Floor, Kirkman House, 12–14 Whitfield Street, London W1P 6AX. Tel. 0171 637 9939.

10. **National Council for Vocational Qualifications**
    222 Euston Road, London NW1 2BZ. Tel. 0171 072 1958.

11. **City and Guilds**
    45 Britannia Street, London WC1X 9RG. Tel. 0171 278 2468.

12. **BTEC**
    Central House, Upper Woburn Place, London WC1H 0HH. Tel. 0171 413 8400.

13. **RSA**
    The GNVQ Unit RSA Examinations Board, Westwood Way, Coventry CV4 8HS. Tel. 01203 470033.

14. **SRCET**
    Mezzanine Suite, PO Box 2055, Civic Offices, Civic Centre, Reading RG1 7ET. Tel. 01734 390592.

15. **SCOTVEC**
    Hanover House, 24 Douglas Street, Glasgow G2 7NQ. Tel. 0141 248 7900.

16. **FEU**
    Spring Gardens, Citadel Place, Tinworth Street, London SE11 5EH. Tel. 0171 962 1280.

17. **ADAR**
    Penn House, 9 Broad Street, Hereford HR4 9AP. Tel. 01432 266653.

Index